ET

DATE DUE

THE HUMAN SIDE OF PLANNING

DAVID W. EWING

The Human Side of Planning

TOOL OR TYRANT?

The Macmillan Company

Collier-Macmillan Ltd., London

TO *My Mother* AND *Father*

Contents

Preface

THIS BOOK is addressed to leaders and would-be leaders in business, government, education, community service, and other fields. Although the nature of their tasks may vary greatly in many respects, these leaders have certain problems in common. Generally they must work through organizations, and their own futures are likely to be dependent in part on the futures of their organizations (and vice versa). Hence it is very important to them to know how to make and implement decisions today that will improve the organization's position tomorrow. Making such decisions is what planning is all about.

Professional planners, too, will be interested in some of the materials presented in this book. I have purposely avoided naming them as *the* audience, however, because the term "planner" is so often used to describe a specialized group of people. And planning, at least as it is conceived of here, is not at all specialized. When a leader makes a decision, he often makes, consciously or unconsciously, one or more assumptions about the future. Moreover, his decision is likely to have implications for the work and hopes of other people in his organization—and their decisions in turn may well affect his projects. As a result, he has a direct and practical interest in the activity I call planning.

Two other audiences for this volume should be mentioned. One consists of the analysts of corporations, those men and women who concern themselves with the probable future ups and downs of a company's stock, value, or position in the market. As George Olmsted, Jr., points out (see page 42), the analyst who concerns himself only with the "figure" aspects of planning gets but part of the story. What about the *people* in the company? What will *they* be doing, and how?

The other audience is made up of legislators and public opinion leaders who seek to evaluate and influence the performance of government agencies. Planning could become, if the American people so desire, a potent tool of public control over national, state, and local governments. If the public demanded that agencies make and disclose long-range programs, which could then be openly discussed, the people could influence the conduct of an administration far more effectively than by punishing or rewarding it, in budget committees or at the polls, for its past performance. Punishments and rewards usually come too late to be effective "discipliners" in the United States political society today. The public is too far removed from government operations, for one thing; there is also the tradition of fixed terms of office, for another. But neither of these factors would keep the public from influencing the choice of long-range programs, if such were disclosed. The public would also gain far better benchmarks for evaluating the quality of performance in the future.

The ideas in this book are based on a variety of experiences. They are based on talks with executives in business, government, and other fields. They are based also on cases (especially some produced at the Harvard Business School), articles, and other accounts of management work. To a certain extent, too, biographies and histories have been used to analyze successes and failures in planning in times past. As a layman, I have tried to base my interpretation of historical events upon research done in a professional manner by others. It was enlightening to find great public and military leaders of the past engaged in much the same struggle to weave together the human and material aspects of planning as are many space-age leaders today.

It has also been rewarding to venture briefly into accounts of planning in the Soviet Union, where the behavioral aspect is conspicuously minimized as a result of the influence of Marxist and Leninist thought. If the concepts advocated in this book have any validity at all, Soviet economic and political planners work under a long-run handicap of very serious proportions, one that will continue to hobble them despite their many technical and intellectual advantages.

The title chosen for this book is, of course, a steal from the great Douglas McGregor's *The Human Side of Enterprise*, published in 1961 by McGraw-Hill Book Company. In fact, McGregor's book helped to suggest a focus for this one at the outset of the writing. Like his volume, this one deals primarily with people's efforts within a productive organization—the quest for teamwork and collaboration—rather than with, say, the human factor in the marketplace or in public relations. Writers have already analyzed such questions as how to make a company's marketing program appealing to potential customers or how to make a government program appealing to the public.

I am indebted to Miss Vicky Boggs and Miss Elizabeth Knox for typing the book manuscript. I am also indebted to a very patient wife who cheerfully put up with many inconveniences so that the writing could go on.

DAVID W. EWING

Boston, Massachusetts

PART 1:

Crises in Concept

CHAPTER 1

Tool for Survival

THE TERM "planning" is an old one. It has been in many languages for a great many centuries—ever since man began thinking of the future implications of current choices of áction. But the connotations of planning have changed. In the beginning, planning was a simple device used by individuals, families, and small groups. When societies became highly organized, however, planning came to be a device of leadership and management. In this sense it took on complexities and subtleties it had never had before.

Equally important, the connotations of planning as a management tool have changed. In times past, planning could be considered a luxury, a useful "extra" in the arsenal of tools used by leaders seeking to bring about change. It gave to the men and institutions employing it—the Hannibals, the Alfred the Greats, the Bismarcks, the East India Companies, the Union Pacific Railroads—valuable advantages in their quests of great goals. However, it could not be called then an indispensable device. More often than not, organizations succeeded without it. Today this is no longer so. We seem to be fast approaching a point at which the very fate of corporations, cities, public-service agencies, military organizations, state governments—and even whole nations and populations—will depend on their leaders' willingness and ability to plan.

This state of affairs could have been predicted long ago. Once the industrial revolution, the population explosion, and certain Western values concerning progress and change became established, it was inevitable that planning would become a necessity, not simply because of growing demands on resources or longer lead times in technology nor because of the fact that people must depend more on each other in modern society. The crucial reason is that *organizations* have come to depend greatly on one another. Once institutions like big government, big labor, big agriculture, big business, and big health and welfare become interdependent, once they begin dividing into numerous subinstitutions—the many agencies in Washington; the chains of national, regional, and local offices in labor; the networks of growers, processors, and the complex teams of contractors, subcontractors, suppliers, and servicers in industry; the innumerable medical, social aid, and administrative units in health and welfare—then planning becomes a condition of existence. The big question in planning becomes not whether it is justified but to what extent and in what manner it shall be practiced.

In the United States, the Department of Defense has become famous for its advancement of the art of planning; former Defense Secretary Robert McNamara's much-discussed planning-programming-budgeting cycle, instituted early in the 1960's, was only one of the department's many achievements in this respect. The National Aeronautics and Space Administration, with its highly publicized programs for exploring the moon, Mars, Venus, and other planets years and decades in the future, has advertised planning with great success. Voluntary health, welfare, and recreation agencies, such as the Camp Fire Girls and the United Seamen's Service, have adopted concepts of planning espoused by the National Budget and Consultation Committee. Universities and colleges have gone seriously into planning. In different parts of the nation, public and private agencies are planning for the development and preservation of resources like water, wildlife, and park lands. Any large city telephone directory contains a number of organizational listings with planning words in the titles. We plan our families. We plan to finance the education of our children.

We plan for our retirement. Estate planning, once an art known only to the elite, is now common in the middle class.

Of especial importance, United States business corporations are doing an increasing amount of short- and long-range planning. A *Business Week* survey of 500 companies in January, 1967, revealed that 71 percent of 139 respondents had formal, organized systems to carry out long-range planning; many of these firms reported having established their systems during the previous few years. And later in 1967 a National Planning Association survey of 1,800 companies, with 420 responding, showed nearly 85 percent preparing long-term plans (well over half of them having started the work after 1960), with more than 50 percent revising their plans annually, and about 25 percent planning ahead for more than the five-year period used by the majority. Further evidence of the growing importance attached to planning comes from a survey conducted in 1967 by the consulting firm of Heidrick and Struggles. The area that currently demanded the most attention, 471 presidents of large companies reported, was planning. (The next two most important areas were marketing and motivating people.)

What has been happening in the United States is also happening in greater or lesser degree in other industrialized nations. Since World War II, France, Belgium, England, the Netherlands, the Scandinavian countries, Red China, India, Pakistan, and other nations have developed planning at the government level. France's so-called indicative planning has received the most attention of the European efforts. The Soviet Union, as everyone knows, was able to transform itself into a modern industrial power in only a few decades with the help of comprehensive five-year plans. Lenin not only formulated the tasks of the Soviet Union's first long-term national economic program (which was for electrification) in 1920, but also gave practical advice on how to draft it;[1] the "dreamer in the Kremlin," as visitor H. G. Wells called him, started a conceptual revolution even though failing to grasp

[1] Mikhail Bor, *Aims and Methods of Soviet Planning* (New York, International Publishers Co., Inc., 1967), p. 22.

the importance of its most important ingredient, the art of management and administration. In other countries, industry, too, has flung itself into the act. Magazines like *International Management* continually report on the planning efforts of a growing number of companies in England, the Netherlands, Italy, Germany, Japan, and other countries. It was a French industrialist, Henri Fayol, who led the first formal, systematic, comprehensive planning that we know of in industry; he called it a "precious instrument" in reversing the fortunes of a collapsing mining and metallurgical concern near the end of the nineteenth century and turning the firm into a large and strong combine.

As might be expected, concepts and definitions of planning vary a great deal. It is fair to generalize, however, that most leaders of private and public organizations consider planning a dynamic tool. It is a means to evolution or revolution, however the need is perceived. It is a method of preparing an organization for a changing future—of so directing, training, and equipping employees that they take the actions today that will advance the organization toward desired new objectives during a stipulated future period. Also, planning usually implies the development of a program for accomplishing a goal and of some kind of system for deciding on ends and means; however, both the program and system may be quite informal.

An inspection of the literature will show definitions that are both more and less precise and more and less ambitious than the foregoing; also, some definitions are far more specialized, reflecting the particular interests of experts (e.g., operations researchers, marketing men). Nevertheless, the description just given captures the essence of planning as many leaders of organizations the world over are trying to put it into practice.

It must be emphasized that planning, as political and industrial leaders usually think of it—and also as it will be considered in this book—is a tool for producing desired *changes* and *transformations* in an organization's structure or manner of operation. Planning, as we shall consider it, has little relevance to organizations seeking only to extend or project their present performance into the future. Let us suppose that a manufacturer of nuts and bolts foresees an increase of 10 percent in the sales of these products and schedules appropriate additions to his staff of clerks and salesmen. This is *not* the kind of activity we refer to. However, if the same manufacturer were to seek to produce and sell new lines of hardware equipment or to change the structure and functions of his organization so it could do the job better, then the activity would come under our purview.

Although planning is the responsibility primarily of management, managers are by no means the only persons with an interest in it. What management does influences the lives and aspirations of individuals and their families. There is no telling how many hundreds of thousands of families owe their happiness or frustrations at least in part to such management practices as planning —probably at least as many families as can thank or blame good or bad education, medical practice, or regional politics. When we consider an advance in the quality of management planning, therefore, we consider also an advance in the quality of living.

Planning has not come into wide practice without resistance. Planners have fought an uphill struggle through most of our history in the United States and in numerous other countries as well —and still are fighting heavy resistance a large part of the time. To many people, planning often smacks of regimentation, authoritarianism, and excessive control. People who share this view are by no means limited to the John Birch Society. A friend of mine in Michigan, a prominent minister with a large, influential, and generally liberal congregation, tells me that he is constantly amazed over the fear and alarm expressed by his parishioners concerning the growth and centralization of planning in government, industry, and the unions. Such antipathy has deep roots. It goes back to colonial times, and it is reflected in one after another of the most precious documents of our governmental and industrial system. Even in the military, until recently, planners were an object of suspicion. When a subordinate officer in the Confederate army asked Stonewall Jackson about his plans for the next few days, Jackson put him under guard. When Woodrow Wilson heard, in August of 1915, that certain military officers in Washington were making plans for conducting a war *if* war should come, Wilson ordered the work stopped and demanded that the officers leave Washington immediately.

Nevertheless, there is practically no period in the history of the United States when it could be said that planning was effectively denied. It has always been a growing thing; it has stubbornly maintained its roots in the consciousness and desires of leaders. Cut it down, burn it, hem it in as its opponents will, they have never been able to destroy it. One of the most ambitious long-range plans ever sponsored by a federal executive in this country was Albert Gallatin's transportation program, which he outlined in 1808, after being instructed by the Senate to draw up such a plan.[2] Gallatin recommended an ingenious and logical system of north-south and east-west connections, including a turnpike from Maine to Georgia that would link all major ports and a network of turnpikes and rivers linking the East and West. He prepared a ten-year schedule of federal appropriations and public works. Gallatin's plan was interrupted by a sharp decline in tax receipts caused by the embargo against France and Britain and by the War of 1812. The plan was never accomplished during his lifetime, but a hundred years later it was achieved. The story mirrors the planning movement in general—endlessly interrupted, frustrated, defeated, yet somehow triumphing in the end. If the movement were given popularity ratings, as television programs are, one of its all-time "lows" would have occurred in the years just before the New Deal. Yet in one of those years, 1931, a committee of the National Progressive Conference published a memorandum on "Long-Range Planning for the Stabilization of Industry"; Gerard Swope of General Electric Company proposed a scheme for industry planning by trade associations and cartels; and the Book-of-the-Month Club offered a book about Russia's planning, M. Ilin's *New Russia's Primer*, which became one of its more popular choices![3]

[2] See George Soule, *Planning U.S.A.* (New York, The Viking Press, 1967), pp. 27–28, and Raymond Walters, Jr., *Albert Gallatin* (New York, The Macmillan Company, 1957), pp. 182–84.

[3] Soule, *op. cit.*, p. 95.

Motives and Incentives

What motives have inspired planners? Some men and women, no doubt, have seen planning as a means to personal power and recognition. A decision to enact a certain program is in effect a decision *not* to support competing programs and interests, with all that means for the struggle for power of rival factions in an organization. Further, officials of the victorious program can use it in an endless variety of subtle ways to feather their political nests. In fact, it is the rare executive who overlooks this aspect completely when he reviews a program, no matter how sincere and competent he or she is. On the other hand, it is surely fair to say that the power motive has not dominated. Planning as a management tool seems to have attracted more than the customary share of idealists and visionaries. One who goes back through the published record gains the impression that, at least in the barrage of attacks and counterattacks over major political plans, Henry Wallace–type idealists have more often been an object of concern than the personal-interest schemers.

Personal wealth and aggrandizement have also motivated some planners. Unfortunately for the "public image" of the movement, a number of the most ingenious programs have been conceived for this reason—Harley's South Sea Scheme ("Bubble") in England in 1711, for instance, and the Crédit Mobilier enterprise that scandalized many businessmen and politicians soon after the Civil War in the United States.

Certainly one of the most important and recurring motives for planning has been the desire for controlling what people do. A long-range military program gives the President some means of controlling what the generals and admirals do; a long-range corporate plan gives directors and stockholders an often effective way of guiding what the professional managers do. It is significant that the push for professional management standards in the field of voluntary health and welfare organizations has been prompted in part by a similar desire. As Earle Lippincott and Elling

Aannestad have eloquently pointed out,[4] the approximately 100,000 voluntary health and welfare agencies in the United States have often sprung up because of the desire of strong individuals to satisfy certain perceived needs, without much attention to whether or not the agency duplicated, or might later duplicate, the work of other agencies. For directors and trustees of such organizations, a specific program with carefully spelled-out goals is an excellent way of assuring that an agency works on a job that needs to be done and of meshing its efforts with the efforts of other agencies that may be performing related tasks. Also, such a program offers trustees a valuable benchmark for evaluating staff operations. A few years ago, Lippincott and Aannestad report, the board of Camp Fire Girls, Inc., worked out a statement of one-year goals that filled more than two pages (e.g., "develop and implement a project for girls in the critical areas of selected metropolitan cities involving expansion of services to the most needy, experimentation, and research"), and the organization's operating executives made up detailed worksheets that were three times as long as the board's, listing how, where, and by whom the goals were to be achieved.

But the area where the control motive is far and away the strongest—or, at least, should be the strongest—is government. For here the public is removed from the day-to-day operating people by such a hopelessly long succession of stages, levels, and buffer groups that, without a set of published programs, it has only the crudest and most sporadic means of guiding what the bureaucracy does. If there is a Marshall Plan, the public can make its voice heard more effectively for and against overseas activities that support or contradict that program. If there is an Alliance for Progress scheme, it expedites public discussion of goals for the various federal agencies working in South and Central America. President Lyndon Johnson's poverty program was a way of effecting a ubiquitous public's will that something more should be done by Washington to help the poor. The many

4 "Management of Voluntary Welfare Agencies," *Harvard Business Review*, November–December, 1964, p. 87.

programs associated with the Employment Act of 1946 are one means available to Congress of making the vast federal bureaucracy, to use the words of the act, "utilize all its plans, functions, and resources for the purpose of creating and maintaining, in a manner calculated to foster and promote free competitive enterprise and the general welfare, conditions under which there will be afforded useful employment opportunities, including self employment, to those able, willing and seeking to work, and to promote maximum employment, production and purchasing power."

Indeed, one may well wonder why Americans have not demanded more planning, not less, from government agencies in order to improve public control of them. It is extremely difficult to tell from the record of results alone whether a particular agency is doing a good job of what it should be doing. It may be giving the public the fast shuffle; it may be producing an excellent temporary showing by using shortcuts that will penalize performance several years later under a different administration. Or it may be doing just the opposite, building for the future without showing quickly recognizable gains today. How can the public tell, with only press reports, officials' television appearances, and budget figures to go on? But if the agency has a program, especially a program that details over a period of time what should be done, and in what manner, in order to accomplish certain objectives, then the citizenry has at least a fighting chance to make its weight felt in the federal and state capitols.

Many of those who have struggled in behalf of the planning movement have another type of motive: more ambitious and stimulating *goals* for organizations. For example, in recent years we have heard much criticism of industry from young people who feel that the corporate purpose is too often pedestrian and stultifying. Planning-minded executives have done better than nonplanners in producing at least a partial answer to this complaint. Planning techniques have helped managers visualize the possibilities of diversification, of broadening not only the product lines a company sells but the fields of business it is in, the kinds of research it supports, and even the areas of the earth in which it operates. Sears, Roebuck could not have launched a revolution in business service in South America without planning; nor could Ralston Purina, Quaker Oats, and other companies be pioneering solutions to food shortages in underdeveloped countries without some sophisticated planning. The same tool has been indispensable to International Business Machines Corporation in helping to bring about the computer revolution, to Lockheed Aircraft and Boeing in speeding the transportation revolution, to First National Stores and A&P in advancing the revolution in food distribution. Some leading insurance companies would not be making news in urban renewal if it were not for planners and planning; nor would certain oil and automotive corporations be making headway in efforts to reduce pollution but for planning. One could go on at some length with such examples.

Still another motive for planning has been its value in increasing *efficiency* and *effectiveness*. It helps to keep an organization on course, to avoid unnecessary backtracking and detour-making, and to arrange the many operations that numerous people undertake in an orderly, productive sequence. The Program Evaluation and Review Technique ("PERT"), one of many planning methods used with great success by the United States Navy, helped that organization develop the Polaris submarine efficiently in an unprecedentedly short time; and a similar technique, the Critical Path Method ("CPM") has helped various industrial organizations to launch new products and services in about one-half of the time that probably would have been required without the method. So priceless is planning in this matter of scheduling and coordination that one large aerospace corporation I know of insists that a member of the planning staff be present at every significant top management meeting and go with headquarters executives on every important trip to meet with division heads and review their operations.

Not the least of many strong motives for supporting planning is its effect on the way *people feel and work together* in an organization. Because the tool is used jointly with other management methods, it is difficult to draw a line and say, "This is a result of planning; that is not." Nevertheless, the careful observer can make reasonable and fact-based judgments concerning the impact on a group of people. This has been done by a Harvard Business School doctoral student with whom I worked, Phillip F. Myers (now a business executive). Myers' doctoral study covers long-range planning in six electronics companies.[5] Some of the companies had a successful, sophisticated planning approach, and some did not, so Myers was able to make revealing comparisons. He found, for one thing, that planning influences morale considerably. Many executives told him planning made them feel more secure, more confident of the company's future, more confident of the management teams they belonged to. As one executive remarked to him, "Did you ever hear of a pessimistic long-range plan?"

Secondly, the study shows that planning has a very heavy impact on methods of evaluating executive performance. Where there is ineffective planning, managers receive little guidance concerning how they or their units are to contribute to their organization's future. They are generally left in the dark about whether they are doing well or not (until the chief executive tells them, if he ever does). But where there is planning, so that organizational objectives can be specified, managers have a clearer, more consistent understanding of how they and their units are to be evaluated. In fact, they can often evaluate their performance by themselves.

Third, the evidence reveals a strong relationship between planning and cooperation among various management groups. Cooperation generally requires that different groups share the same goals and ideas about broad programs. This is feasible if there is planning, but extremely difficult without it. In the absence of planning, and hence of a general consensus on organizational objectives, misunderstanding of purpose comes all too easily. Fur-

[5] "A Comparative Study of Long-Range Planning and Its Influences on the Management Practices of Several Large Electronics Companies" (Ph.D. dissertation, Harvard Business School, 1966).

thermore, there is preoccupation with current crises, with "fire fighting," and this, too, tends to upset the possibilities of cooperation and coordination. Myers adds:

> Several executives explained how, in the low planning environments, different executives would develop their own plans or no plans at all. When one executive wished to secure the cooperation of another, he frequently had to try to convince the others of the appropriateness of his own plan. But this was reported to be extremely difficult to do in general, particularly when two plans differed. Not infrequently, different executives or groups would be working on their own plans without knowledge of the plans of others.

Fourth, and perhaps most significant of all, Myers' case studies indicate that planning has a powerful and unique effect on the general quality of management practice in an organization. While influence here is circular, with general management affecting planning as well as vice versa, Myers' evidence suggests that planning is probably more important as a cause of good management than as an effect. For instance, one of the companies studied had virtually no planning for many years; then, after the firm ran into serious financial troubles, a new president took over and injected heavy doses of planning into management activity. Subsequently, the quality of management practices in general began to improve noticeably. Executives began working together better and with more sophistication in a great many ways, large and small, in marketing, procurement, manufacturing, finance, industrial relations, and other areas. Planning appeared to be the principal cause of the change. Knowing what was coming next for the organization and no longer having to live hand to mouth, executives found it possible to work in a manner previously deemed impossible. Myers concludes:

> We know of no other factor of near the significance of planning which could have so directly induced a change in behavior of the magnitude observed. The data would suggest that the directness and influence of planning on management practices was very substantial indeed, and that changes up or down in planning would result in very significant changes in management practices. . . . There definitely appeared to be a lag in change of management practices, from the

onset of increased planning efforts. The data indicate this lag is probably from one to three years.

In addition to the benefits Myers describes, planning appears to have a visible impact on the quality of human relations in an organization. Surely it is no major solution to the interpersonal woes that crop up whenever people work together; certainly, too, it is no reliever of tension. What can legitimately be claimed, however, is that planning tends to produce more constructive varieties of friction and tension—the kinds that come from struggling for common purposes and in a more or less rational manner, instead of the ones that come from internecine "me against you" contests when there is no visible set of purposes and programs. While the transformation is subtle on a day-to-day basis, it can be spectacular over a period of time. In the words of a man I once talked to who had experienced the change, it "was like a great fog lifting."

In the affluent economies of today, the motives to plan are stronger than ever, and they are resulting in an enormous increase in the number of planning efforts in public and private organizations of all types. At the same time, increasing sophistication in planning is often giving the organizations that employ it major advantages over those that do not. These two trends, working simultaneously and each reinforcing the other, have significance for leaders and aspirants to leadership in numerous fields. In the highly competitive arena of private industry, planning is on the way to becoming a condition of staying in the race. In government, an agency's or administration's chances of measuring up in the harsh light of public scrutiny are better if it plans—and plans well. In education, in the voluntary health and welfare field, and in other civic endeavors, planning is becoming a tool that *must* be used if an organization is to live up to people's expectations.

I HOLD that man is in the right who is most in league with the future.
                                                    —HENRIK IBSEN

CHAPTER 2

Fiascos and Frustrations

THE PARADOX is that the planning movement, despite such strong motives to make it succeed, has not generally been blessed with success. The triumphs have been stunning—but few. Sophistication has increased—but not nearly so much as leaders have wished it would. An alarmingly high failure rate has characterized the past efforts of executives in industry, government, the military, and education. It is difficult to be precise about the failure rate; we have no scholarly studies available that use a careful definition of "failure," cover a sufficient sample of organizations over a sufficiently long period of time, or make appropriate allowances for the many exogenous factors outside the planners' control which may cause failure. We must, therefore, rely on general impressions and observations. These seem to leave little doubt that plans and programs—at least, those of significance in terms of investment, objectives sought, and the amount of change desired—have failed at least as often as they have succeeded, and probably more.

For example, one management consultant I know—a man who has worked closely with planners in many different fields of work—tells me that "over half" of the plans he has observed have failed to achieve the intended goals. I have queried a number of businessmen on this question; their consensus is that the "majority" of programs fall far short of the mark or are discarded. According to a group of knowledgeable government executives in Washington whom I have interviewed, "most" planning attempts fail. One can take his choice of such opinions; all of them point in the same general direction. My own judgment is that (a) if failure is defined to include programs shelved, drastically revised, or productive of results considerably less than was intended (in terms of profit, sales, benefits conferred, performance standards, building deadlines, etc.), as well as outright fiascos (the marketing bust of the Edsel, for instance, or some of the "pacification" programs in Vietnam), and (b) if program failures that are clearly due to noncontrollable factors are excluded (for instance, a corporate acquisition program thwarted by the antitrust department or a highway program suspended because of war), and (c) if the plans considered are limited to those that seek to produce some kind of significant change—then the failure rate for United States organizations must be running somewhere between 50 and 80 percent in any major area like industry, government, or education.

Although many planning failures are carefully concealed from the outside world by top management, numerous others are conspicuous enough to become the subjects of common talk. Quite often this is the case in community programs. As an illustration, Irwin T. Sanders, an executive of the Ford Foundation at the time of this incident, reports that about fifty or sixty members of local boards and organizations of a city were once invited to a high school auditorium where they were told they would be given some interesting material about which their opinions would be sought. When they arrived in the auditorium, a plan for the city was distributed to them (this was not a complete surprise, because the news had earlier gone along the grapevine). It was a comprehensive program—beautifully prepared, done by an architect and his firm, and financed by a bank for some $20,000. The planners in charge of the meeting wanted the persons present to endorse the program so it could be sent to the proper political agencies for implementation. The people at the meeting were generally sympathetic to the program idea, but they soon learned, after the questions started, that the planning leaders had not yet consulted the city-county planning commission. Once that information was disclosed, the program was as good as dead. The plan books just gathered dust (although some people kept them for certain data contained), the community gave no subsequent support, and there was no progress in implementation.[1]

One of the most decisive failures I know about in industry happened to a sizable electronics corporation in the late 1950's.[2] Sensing the need for revitalizing the company, top executives set in motion a planning program that was second to none in meticulous detail. First they appointed a corporate director of long-range planning and gave him the assignment of drafting a program for planning and budgeting in five-year cycles. He put together a document that he called "Plan for Planning." This tome proposed policies and reports to be gathered, outlined details of data gathering, specified various executives' responsibilities, outlined working relationships and other matters. For instance, it specified the six officers who should compose the division planning committee of a division, the twelve main duties of this committee, and the subduties of some of the main duties.

The "Plan for Planning" was approved and a corporate planning committee formally established. Paper began to fly from headquarters. The corporate divisions were instructed to begin preparing tentative and final plans. Some submitted good ones, some poor ones. Many division managers complained bitterly. One said that his plan had required forty-five man-months of work. He didn't see how top management could possibly read his report, it was so voluminous.

After the division plans were sent to headquarters, the managers waited expectantly for feedback. In most cases it never came. "You submit a plan," one division manager complained, "and don't hear very much from then on. All they tell you is whether the division's budget has been accepted or not." He added, "We

[1] See Robert Morris (ed.), *Centrally Planned Change: Prospects and Concepts* (New York, National Association of Social Workers, 1964).
[2] For the facts of this case, the identity of which cannot be revealed, I am indebted to Harbridge House, Inc., Boston, Mass.

get a few memos about specifics and we pick up things on the grapevine, but I've never seen any formal statement from top management."

The indefatigable planning director, with the approval of the president, then drafted a memo to standardize the form and content of plans submitted by division heads. There were to be twelve section headings in a plan, and careful distinctions were specified between short-term and long-term anticipations, new and old products, different problem areas, financial objectives, and other matters. This paper, like its predecessors, was a masterpiece of detail.

But this burst of effort, like the last flamboyant display of rocketry in a Fourth of July display, was to signal the end. The executive vice-president responsible for appointing the planning director resigned from the company, the planning director was shipped off to another job, and the post of planning director was left unfilled. Presumably, with the spectre of planning gone, more than one division head slept peacefully for the first time in many months.

Failures like the foregoing are not unusual in industry; there is evidence of them in numerous business school cases, annual reports, and files of consultants. For sheer magnitude of fiasco, however, business cannot compete with planners in the military and government. Witness the frustrations of the "Pacification Program" in Vietnam, some of the Johnson Administration's "War on Poverty" programs, and state financial crises with Medicaid in late 1967 and in 1968.

Sometimes it is assumed that such boners are the work principally of amateurs—executives and administrators who do not consider themselves specialists in planning. Would that it were so! Indeed, I have heard knowledgeable people argue that egregious errors are made more often, not less, by the full-time professionals. Favorite examples are eight-lane freeways that cut through the middles of homogeneous communities, urban renewal programs that helped the well-to-do more than the poor, foreign agricultural assistance programs memorialized by expensive tractors and combines rusting away in the undergrowth because nobody knew how to use them, and, in industry, such immortal fiascos in marketing planning as the ill-fated Edsel—all the work in large part of "experts" in the trade. While the contention would be difficult to prove, one thing does seem abundantly clear: the professionals have not profited from past case experience in the manner that, say, doctors or engineers have learned from experience.

To cite but one example, in 1880, George Pullman's team of city planners built a model town for employees of the Pullman Palace Car Company and other factories; millions of dollars were spent to produce an efficient, aesthetic, orderly, culture-rich, sound community that would be a joy for industrial workers to live in. The model town was engineered, constructed, and managed with idealistic care—but workers hated it, the town went to pot, and by 1910 the company had sold off the property after suffering enormous losses. One would think the many corporate planners since then would have learned quickly from this sobering experience; the reasons for failure were quite apparent, and surely the case would seem to merit the attention of specialists giving full time to planning assignments. Yet the planning blunders that doomed Pullman, Illinois, have been repeated regularly in this century by designers of company towns and new cities. Some brilliant exceptions to the rule may be in the making—one is probably Columbia, Maryland, being created by combinations of private capital—but they seem to be few in number and, more important, most professional planners do not even seem to be aware that such a case as Pullman exists.[3]

Lest the impression be given here that United States agencies and companies have failed more conspicuously than organizations in other countries, let us turn briefly to the world's most publicized group of planners, the Soviets. Planning failures in the Soviet Union are especially noteworthy because this nation has certain enormous advantages. It has perhaps the longest experience

[3] For a good account, see Stanley Buder, *Pullman* (New York, Oxford University Press, 1967).

with comprehensive economic planning, and such planning enjoys 100 percent backing from the top of the hierarchy; the first comprehensive economic plan, Gosplan, was launched in 1921 with Lenin's full participation and support, and succeeding plans have had similar support from Stalin, Khrushchev, and the current regime. Moreover, the Soviets have assigned many of their most brilliant men and women to planning—and imposed extremely harsh penalties on those officials and managers down the line who failed to meet planned targets. Judging from statements I have heard many times at meetings of planners, advantages like these *should* make planning nigh infallible!

But such is not the case. It is true that the Soviet Union made dramatic progress and that planning gets much of the credit for this progress. Nevertheless, Russian planning has been riddled with serious failure—in agriculture, in manufacturing, in transportation, in distribution, and in many other fields. And some of the most spectacular errors, there is good reason to believe, are in the making today (e.g., plunging into the manufacture of automobiles without simultaneous, comparably ambitious investments in road building). This judgment can be softened somewhat by acknowledging that a good proportion of the debacles have been in long-range programs, which are especially vulnerable to hazards beyond leaders' control. Yet a look at planning periods that *are* short enough to establish accountability will show similarly discouraging results. This was true, for example, in the case of a cable plant in 1964 and 1965. Typical of many experiences before and since, this case was described by L. Kazlov, assistant director of the plant, in the May 12, 1965, issue of *Pravda*.

In 1964 the managers of the Odessa Cable Plant, which had an important role to play in its industry's program, waited expectantly for a production plan to come through planning agency channels. Not until late in the year, however, did the document actually come into their hands. The plant managers had overoptimistically *thought* it was late in coming to them because of an extra careful review by the planning authority, but this turned out not to be the case. For instance, Kazlov reports, they soon saw to their dismay that they would get less polyvinyl chloride plastic, their basic raw material, than they would have to have to meet the planned output quota. Right away they "rang all the alarms." They searched to see who was at fault for the error. After hunting through "mountains of paper," they finally found the culprit—one T. N. Lyobimova, the Ukraine Economic Council's chief specialist for the cable industry. When they went to see her, there were no denials or excuses. She did make it clear, however, that any correction would have to come from a higher agency. "Go to Moscow and see what you can do there" was the advice.

So the Odessa Cable managers did that, Kazlov reports. They made the rounds of dozens of offices of numerous organizations. Their case seemed like a very simple and obvious one to present: to produce the planned output, they needed a certain amount of raw materials, but they were not scheduled to receive that amount and hence could not produce the output unless changes were made. "Are we supposed to make polyvinyl chloride out of air?" the operating managers asked the economic planners. They visited and visited, talked and talked, pleaded and cajoled, and got plenty of sympathy but no action. A curious explanation for inaction was given to them: if the Odessa plant did not produce its quota of cable, explained the planners, the construction of many important projects in the Soviet Union and the manufacture of some important machines would be disrupted.

Why not look into the possibilities for getting more plastic? With time running out on them and the tension steadily growing (personal liberty could be at stake, as well as the plant's status), the plant managers dashed for a train to the Vladimir Chemical Plant. But any hopes they had for finding a solution there were short-lived. The Vladimir outfit, they soon learned, was already overloaded. In fact, Kazlov reports, the demand for every last drop of Vladimir's plastic output was so great that the stuff was "taken still warm directly from the machines, snatched up by the representatives of nearby cable plants and carried off to their enterprises."

One thing became starkly clear: the plan for industrial cable production was not going to work!

Is So Much Failure Necessary?

It can be argued that a high failure rate is inevitable, that planning cannot be compared fairly with other management functions subject to less failure because it is inherently liable to error. There is indeed an implied risk in planning for change that does not lie in, say, budgeting or purchasing, which are tied more to known facts and the continuation of familiar operations. In fact, many plans are subject to a conspicuously high degree of risk—and this is done on purpose by the planning leaders. Also, as earlier indicated, over many programs hangs the cloud of uncontrollable events—the unexpected war, the technological breakthrough that no forecaster could anticipate, the accidental death or sickness of key people. Even if the event itself never materializes, the ever-present threat of it may well handicap planners in a psychological way, just as the threat of a thundershower may throw a golfer off his game even though no drop of rain ever falls.

Nevertheless, when due allowance is made for such matters, there are strong reasons for believing that many of the failures —two-thirds of them, perhaps—are *not* inevitable. One reason for this belief is that many organizations that began with a poor record have steadily improved their batting average (without diminishing the ambitiousness or riskiness of their programs); the electronics company earlier mentioned, for example, now scores many successes as a result of its planning effort. Such cases are evidence that management groups can *learn* how to circumvent many of the pitfalls.

Another reason is that some of the more spectacular successes with planning have taken place in circumstances in which the difficulties were just as great as in the cases of failure. The Soviet space program, a stunning triumph in long-range planning, has been up against all of the obstacles and more that have been used endlessly as excuses by the not-so-successful heads of certain economic ventures. Again, in United States industry, forecasting uncertainty is an old excuse for poor planning in many companies, but no company faces more such uncertainties than Lockheed Aircraft in the aerospace industry, and it has scored some magnificent successes with its planning. And at least one of the successful organization programs undertaken by American labor unions in the past decade was in an area (Southeast Asia) where the difficulties hardly could have been greater. Exceptional luck and managerial brilliance may explain a number of these cases, but by no means all of them.

A third reason for believing that the high failure rate is unnecessary is evidence such as that to be adduced in later sections of this book. This evidence shows that to a large extent both successful and unsuccessful planning can be attributed to causes that are well within man's power to manipulate.

HE WHO can see three days ahead will be rich for three thousand years.

—JAPANESE PROVERB

CHAPTER 3

Where Has Planning Gone Wrong?

OVER A DECADE AGO one of the intellectual leaders in the planning movement, H. Edward Wrapp, made an observation that checked closely with the experience of many executives. "The most serious obstacle to long-range planning," Wrapp stated, after reviewing the difficulties, "is not so much the drain on management time, the actual problems of doing good planning, or the danger of revealing company strategy, as it is the subtle, but occasionally open, opposition of some executives which appears in the early stages of development."[1]

Wrapp's experience was principally in industry. Observers of planning in government organizations, too, have frequently placed the blame for failure on human factors. Irwin T. Sanders, for instance, sees many a career administrator as his own worst enemy in the planning process because he has learned to think of his role in terms of efficiency norms and routinized procedures instead of flexible improvisation to planning experience.[2] He has been taught administration as the science of budget making, delegation of responsibility and personnel management rather than as the art of leading a human organization to respond creatively to changing community conditions.

[1] "Organization for Long-Range Planning," *Harvard Business Review,* January–February, 1957, p. 39.
[2] See Morris (ed.), *op. cit.,* p. 113.

To men and women who are entrusted with the job of making planning work it must therefore seem almost incredible that little attention has been paid to the human factor. At meetings of experts on planning the problem is hardly ever discussed. In past books and articles on planning there is practically no helpful information on this topic (unless bland generalities can be called helpful). Almost all of the emphasis is on formal organization, the role of computers, reporting methods, criteria for evaluating progress, mergers and acquisitions, and so forth. These are vital; no one can properly dispute that. But it is *people* who make planning work. It is for the benefit of *people* that plans and programs are designed in the first place. One is reminded of those periods in the history of Anglo-American law when the jurists and barristers, in their preoccupation with legalistic technicalities, forgot that the basic intent of their profession was to help individuals and families.

Obstacles to the Human Side of Planning

Why do we overlook the human side in planning when we do not in other aspects of management? In marketing, over the years, considerable attention has been given to such topics as salesmen motivation, personal leadership of sales executives, and group collaboration. In production we have built up a rich fund of knowledge of group dynamics. In the literature on control there has long been generous recognition of the human relations dimension. Yet in planning, which is also permeated by questions of organizational behavior, the "people problems" are glossed over. This statement can be supported not only by examination of the literature and agenda of meetings, but also by the practice of corporate planning departments. Late in 1966 the National Industrial Conference Board inquired into the activities of long-range planning units in a cross section of United States manufacturing companies. The respondents indicated that their planning departments collected and analyzed data, disseminated information, proposed corporate goals, and worked on programs for the expansion of facilities, mergers and acquisitions, product diversification, and other such tasks. But none of them reportedly paid regular attention to the human side—to the questions, for instance, of how to assure that plans were carried out enthusiastically by employees or of how to keep programs flexible and adaptable to the changing desires of the human organization.

Similarly, in government programs—including, ironically enough, those most plainly intended by legislators to serve social goals—the preoccupation of staff planners seems almost always to be with physical tasks, political power problems, and procedural matters. One of the few notable exceptions to this rule is the "model cities" concept of urban renewal, wherein much of the responsibility for planning a renewal project is entrusted to the people in the area to be improved. (Also, as certain fathers of the concept foresaw, the "people problems" of urban renewal institutions are crucial.) Even scholars have apparently forgotten the behavioral factors. One can go through a large library of public administration and find few or no serious discussions, cases, or analyses of the human side of, say, highway planning, or public housing programs, or health and welfare planning.

What obsessions and preoccupations have led planners to neglect the "people" aspects? And how have these tendencies hurt the effectiveness of planning? For convenience, I have grouped the obsessions in five categories.

I. BLOODLESS CRITERIA

Obsession Number One has been physical facilities and programs. Planners in education have been obsessed with such matters as buildings, classrooms, student numbers, and costs; governmental planners with such matters as violations prosecuted, areas served, and budgets; industrial planners with such factors as product lines, plant facilities, return-on-investment ratios, and diversification programs.

A superb job has been done of formulating these physical

problems in the most meaningful way for planners and of devising methods of analyzing them effectively. One of the strengths of such work is its great legacy from the past. It is not generally realized that some of the approaches predate the "Age of Mc-Namara" in the Pentagon, modern control and finance courses in business schools, and the contemporary classics on managerial economics. My friend David Novick of the RAND Corporation, himself a leader in governmental planning, states that in 1959, after he had been writing about the planning-programming-budgeting system ("PPBS") for five years, a visitor came to his office who said that he had recently become familiar with Novick's proposals in this area. The visitor thought his experience along the same lines would interest Novick. The visitor showed a set of budget and finance procedures that General Motors had worked out in 1924, which employed concepts very much like the program budget system introduced by the federal government in 1965 (often called a "revolutionary" development). Moreover, before General Motors instituted the procedures, the man said, DuPont had been using them; DuPont introduced them to Alfred Sloan's organization after investing in it early in the 1920's. The visitor was Donaldson Brown, who, before his retirement, was chief financial officer of General Motors and a member of the board of DuPont.

The fact that the physical side of planning has been pursued so vigorously and efficiently and the fact that the human side has not been aggressively pursued have combined to produce a lopsided emphasis in practice. In nearly all companies in which planning is done, managers seek to achieve end results measured in terms of earnings, production volume, payroll, inventories, and so forth. Very few specify the kinds of relationships, incentives, and adjustments that the human organization must make in order to achieve the physical results desired.

Not surprisingly, therefore, managers think in terms of the bloodless criteria when they think of their role in planning, and in their efforts to make a good showing according to those criteria (with all that a good showing means for promotion, bonuses, and so forth) they may find it all too tempting to exploit the human assets. They may shortchange the department or division they work for by cutting down training costs, reducing the time supervisors can afford to spend with subordinates, or neglecting channels of communication and understanding—knowing full well they will be promoted to some other part of the organization before their acts of exploitation "catch up with them." These managers may be aware, at the time of an emergency need for belt-tightening, that it would make more sense in the long run to liquidate $5,000 worth of inventory at half price than lose (or fail to acquire) $50,000 worth of bright young talent that the staff should have. But the inventory slash will soil the profit-and-loss statement immediately, whereas the talent loss will not show up until later, so they will choose the latter.

One of the leaders in efforts to combat this tendency is Rensis Likert, director of the Institute for Social Research at the University of Michigan. Likert is encouraging companies to obtain periodic measurements of the quality of their human organization (feelings of responsibility, attitudes toward supervisors, loyalty, etc.). He tells me that he knows of a few companies that are now procuring such measures, and he believes that we are on the threshold of a sizable increase in the number of such firms.

Unfortunately, managers seeking to bring more balance into their planning will not find a flood of experts ready to help them. Just as in estate planning, when seeking professional help, one's chances seem to be much better than even of landing an adviser whose expertise is helping him minimize taxes by dodging in and out of the tax laws and regulations, rather than finding the measures that will best provide for his family, so, in management, the executive will find the experts generally more interested in helping him manipulate the physical side than providing for the human side.

A wonderful case in point is an episode in a company disguised as "American Radiatronics Corporation."[3] An industrial engineer

---

[3] From a case under this name copyrighted in 1960 by the President and Fellows of Harvard College. Part (A) is referred to here. The case is discussed at greater length in my book, *The Managerial Mind* (New York, The Free Press, 1964), pp. 162–163.

is asked to give his reactions to the operations of a controversial production department in the company. While the department has a superb record of profit contribution and quality (one of the finest such records in the corporation), it is managed by a foreman who gives the operators an unusual amount of latitude to plan and work out their own assembly and testing methods. It does not bother this foreman that there is a messiness and appearance of disorganization in the shop, so long as that does not bother the operators or keep them from meeting ever-rising targets of quality and volume.

The industrial engineer, however, is not nearly so interested in the personal dynamism here as in its physical imperfections. "We've got plans in the works for taking on this place and really making it over," he tells a case writer from outside the company. "This place has never been under engineering control. . . . The first thing we would do if we could get hold of this room would be to put every operation under close engineering surveillance. The whole setup needs to be revamped and overhauled from one end to the other. We'll do it, too. You won't recognize it two years from now. Some of the new products we have in mind will call for a level of sophistication in production methods, equipment design, and cleanliness that'll make this look sick. You've seen pictures of how some of those production departments look in other companies—cleanliness precautions that make them look like operating rooms, temperature and humidity controls, all white painted walls and equipment. That's what we'll have here."

The industrial engineer mentioned is not alone in his myopia. The operations research expert, while taking a broader and perhaps more sophisticated view of the planning process, has an equally severe case. Time and again we hear of instances in which the operations research group, whether an in-house team or from an outside consulting firm, gathers under its collective arm all the quantitative data on a planning question and then goes off and shuts the door behind it to work out a solution.[4] Surrounding

[4] See, for instance, Pearson Hunt, "The Fallacy of the One Big Brain," *Harvard Business Review*, July–August, 1966.

itself with chart paper, slide rules, and computer programs, it identifies the significant variables, classifies different possible future conditions, assigns probabilities to the conditions, calculates returns, and produces a recommendation. All this time, however, it scarcely thinks to interview operating executives, get to know them, and explore with them the assumptions and conditions that will make a recommendation acceptable to them, the ones who must *live* with it. (For example, the operations researcher may blithely assume that profit maximization is the goal of every program, whereas managers in charge of a project frequently do not want to accept the personal risks that profit maximization goals imply.) As a result, the study often is discredited and gathers dust.

If Americans are prone to overemphasize the physical aspects of planning, the Soviets are even worse. They are the world's prime example of preoccupation with mathematical methods and electronic computers as a means of solving planning programs. The emphasis accorded in 1964 to the Unified Automatic System of Management is a case in point. The authors of this system visualized a network of relay posts and computing centers, interconnected and communicating with enterprises, which would process data for economic programs. The hope was "to form an automatic flow of information from base to center, thereby ensuring immediate control over execution of the plan and, in case of need, preparation of required corrections and adjustments in essential elements of the plan."[5] The computing centers were to be installed in Belorussia, Lithuania, the Tartar Autonomous Republic, and the Kiev region. The planners foresaw virtually unlimited gains from this data-processing network. While readers of the Soviet press may have noted frustrated protests by some Russians at the naivity of supposing the technometric approach is the secret to success, the critics' voices seem to have been lost in the shuffle. Yet, judging from the available evidence, there seems to be little doubt that the technometric approach accounts for much of the weakness of Soviet planning today.

[5] Eugene Zaleski, *Planning Reforms in the Soviet Union, 1962–1966* (Chapel Hill, University of North Carolina Press, 1967), p. 56.

2. "OTHER-DIRECTEDNESS"

One of the dominant characteristics of the planning movement is its tremendous emphasis on the external environment of a company or institution. Obsession Number Two, therefore, is demand forecasts, economic conditions, industry trends, population trends, style trends, technological developments, and so forth. Planners tend to look on these factors as "givens" in the strategic problems they try to solve, forgetting that able, purposeful people can *change* the external environment by the actions and programs they undertake.

Thanks to influential writers like Theodore Levitt and Peter Drucker, managers throughout the country are well aware of the dangers of going too far in the opposite direction and actually neglecting the environment. The popularity of the term "marketing myopia," used to describe this error, attests to widespread recognition that a company wedded to a particular product or service has a murderess for a wife. No manufacturer today, no utility, no banker, no retailer, no government agency, no college, no military unit, no health and welfare agency can count on its business or precise function staying the same for long. People's basic needs for transportation, energy, shelter, food, regulatory protection, education, defense, and charity may continue indefinitely, but the specific products and services that meet these needs keep changing.

Still, it is illogical to jump from this concept to the notion that, as one authority has put it, "Planning . . . depends on our ability to predict the shape of things to come," or, as an industrial expert has stated it, "Business planning starts with marketing planning." These notions are to the organization what the psychologist's concept of "other-directedness" is to the individual. They lead to a quality of sameness in policy rather than uniqueness and individuality. Corporations, forecasting the same trends in demand, tend to move in the same direction, and although the move might have been right for a few companies, it cannot be right for many because there is not enough opportunity to go around.

To illustrate, the once bright potentials of the petrochemical industry were ruined for many entrants by a competitive mob, some playing "follow the leader" and others moving in response to original forecasts. Another case in point comes from the distilling industry. A few years ago, Seagram Distillers Company correctly foresaw a public desire to experiment with a wider range of expensive beverages. So Seagram, a company that had once boasted of having only three brands in its line, came out with several new products. The demand turned out to be there, just as predicted—but turning up to meet it with Seagram were a number of competitors motivated by similar forecasts. Moaned one top executive: "Competition is fantastic now. It's just plain murder." By no means did all of those competitors possess the wherewithal to survive.

But the most serious error of "other-directed" planning is that it leads the organization into activities for which it has only average, or possibly below average, ability. Admittedly, almost every leading proponent of the marketing-first school points out that, before management commits itself to a strategy based on analyses of external trends, needs, or opportunities, it should check to be sure that the organization is qualified to carry out the course of action. The trouble is that this sequence of thought gives too low a priority to self-analysis and introspection; the psychology of reasoning in this way is such that the organization is seen to be qualified if it measures up in only a general or average way. To refer back to the petrochemical illustration, almost any oil company could correctly conclude that it had the *general* qualifications needed for petrochemicals, which are related to petroleum technology; and in the distillers example, any of the beverage companies could correctly conclude that it had the *general* aptitudes and experience necessary for success in the "fashion" drinks field.

General qualifications are not enough. In the affluent, highly competitive economies of the West, an increasingly high percentage of consumer activity reflects relatively unpredictable consumer discretion, impulse buying, and subjective choice (whether to buy a backyard swimming pool or take a vacation in Canada, whether to invest one's leisure time in "going back to college" or installing a make-it-yourself stereo set, etc.). In these circumstances, success in corporate life goes more and more to the organization that can perform a task with *superior* ability. Being "average" can be a very risky business, even in fast-expanding markets. An analogy with individual career planning is readily seen. A "fair" engineer is lost in the mob; an "average" advertising copywriter is just another name; an editor who is simply "literate" and "informed" can, if he has influence, cause the downfall of his department; a professional golfer who is less than top-notch had best not waste his time on the tournament circuit with all its Jack Nicklauses, Arnold Palmers, Gary Players, Bobby Nicholses, and other excellent pro players.

3. HUMAN ENGINEERING APPROACH

Sometimes planning has gone wrong, not because it was oblivious to the human side, but because it approached the human aspects in the wrong way. The most common error of this sort is that people can be "engineered" or that there is a "science" of marshaling enthusiasm and cooperation. Let us call this error Obsession Number Three.

The human relations movement of the 1940's and 1950's—at least, as it was often conceived at the time—took the view that management could get employees to do what it wanted them to do if it treated them in certain ways. (Some pioneers in the field, such as Fritz J. Roethlisberger and William F. Whyte of Cornell, strenuously objected to this notion.) This approach infected planning as well as other branches of administration. The manager, some planners assumed, could get subordinates to support his programs if he was "nice" enough to them. Or, other planners assumed, he could get his programs implemented effectively if he could find out who the informal groups and leaders were and motivate them to support the plan.

In recent decades we have also heard often from social scientists, sociometricians, and public relations experts who feel that the key is breaking down the power structure of an organization into its component parts, much as a machine might be broken down, and so arranging and lubricating the parts that it works in a predesigned way. The parts are called the "influentials," the "decision makers," the "power elite," and other such names of roles. William H. Form, a professor at Michigan State University, has commented on this approach as follows: "Educators, welfare workers, journalists, and others enthusiastically plunged into the murky waters of social research. They thought they had found the formula: locate the influentials, sell them your program, and achieve your goals. They, too, soon found that power was a much more complex phenomenon than they had believed. Many so-called influentials were found to be nonunited, not involved, not informed, not interested, and even not influential in basic community decisions."[6]

The Soviet Union has practiced another variation of "human engineering." Its view is that if officials and workers are motivated by common ideals of society, they will fall into line with the planners once programs are announced and explained. With the sincerest of intentions, therefore, top officials in the Soviet Union have talked of "bringing planning to the people" and planning "for" the local agency or factory, meaning in reality that they are sending directives down to local officials, with eager compliance expected as a matter of course. Because the good intentions of central planners are seen as being identical with the will of the workers, the real focus of attention again becomes the technical, the economic, the formal organizational side of the picture. For example, planners have sought to improve the productivity of backward *kolkhozes* (farms) by seemingly endless reorganizations and mergers. Formal authorities, command relationships, standards, quotas, and other rules may be changed with incredible frequency during the course of a planning period—with little or no attention to working with the people on the farms, strengthening their incentives, training them, helping them adjust to change, or making their jobs more satisfying.[7]

[6] "Social Power and Social Welfare," in Morris (ed.), *op. cit.*
[7] See, for instance, the plea by A. Krayeva, an economist, in *Partiynaya Zhizn'*, No. 10, 1965, pp. 20-25.

This version of "human engineering" has worked little better for the Soviets than it has worked either for the many American community organizations which have assumed that, because they have had high ideals of public service, the programs endorsed by directors would automatically be endorsed enthusiastically by workers, or for the English companies which have apparently assumed that, because England's survival so obviously depends on its export ability, every employee would work hard and efficiently on the programs designated by top management.

There seems to be a fatal tendency on the part of "human engineers" to take for granted that the many things they do to motivate the rank and file are as impressive on the receiving end as on the giving end. In actuality, the rank-and-file worker may feel just the opposite. To him there may seem to be practically no careful social engineering at all, just directives and impersonality. Irwin T. Sanders, whose interesting discussion has been mentioned earlier, tells about a talk he had with a community leader working for a state health department. The local man was disgusted; he intended to leave his job soon. "I get a postcard saying that somebody from the State Health Department is going to be in the community on such-and-such a date," he said, "and we are supposed to come together; the health worker then comes and tells us what we are supposed to do. He or she doesn't want to listen to what we say. They are just here to tell us what to do." The community leader added: "I have got better things to do with my time than going there and simply being used by these people trying to carry out something they may think very worthwhile, but which doesn't interest me."[8] Although I don't know this to be true for a fact, I would guess that the officials of the state agency believed they had done a great deal to make people like this community leader feel "involved" in the planning process.

4. THE BLUEPRINT FALLACY

Another pitfall for planners dates back to the socialist movement, perhaps before. The socialists looked at planning as a device

[8] Morris (ed.), *op. cit.*, p. 111.

for fixing the future. Deciding on a program of action was tantamount to settling a series of questions concerning who should do what, how, and when. Basic assumptions and viewpoints became fixed.

From the vantage point of the planning technician or the intellectual, this is a satisfying approach. But it has rarely met the needs of persons involved in carrying out plans and programs, to say nothing of the interests of the intended beneficiaries. What these people generally prefer is flexibility. Without options and choices at different points along the way, they have little opportunity to use initiative or to adapt to changing desires and conditions.

Few notions about planning have more antagonized individualists than this idea—Obsession Number Four—that the future could be blueprinted. In American politics it underlay part of the anti–New Deal philosophy of conservative Republicans like Borah, Landon, and Vandenburg. In American industry businessmen have vociferously objected to any management approach that would limit their freedom of action in the future. In England, Winston Churchill's famous antipathy to planning was due in part to his associating it with the socialist concept. Harking back to an attempt to plan military operations in Southeast Asia during World War II, one of Churchill's military lieutenants wrote:

Winston was by now revolving around the northern end of Sumatra as he had done over Trondheim in the past. He had found with a pair of dividers that we could bomb Singapore from this point and he had set his heart on going there. It was not a suitable base for further operations against Malaya, but I could not get any definite reply from him as to what he hoped to accomplish from there. When I drew his attention to the fact that when he put his left foot down he should know where the right foot was going to, he shook his fist in my face, saying, "I do not want any of your long-term projects, they cripple initiative!" I agreed that they did hamper initiative, but told him that I could not look upon knowing where our next step was going as constituting a long-term project. I told him he must know where he was going, to which he replied that he did not want to know.[9]

[9] Arthur Bryant, *The Turn of the Tide: A History of the War Years Based on the Diaries of Field-Marshall Lord Alan Brooke, Chief of the*

Unfortunately the blueprint notion persists today in many plan-ing councils (although rarely does a planner ever *say* now that a proposed program fixes the future). It continues to account for considerable uneasiness about planning. Significantly, severe critics of the notion can point to some very competent planners in their ranks. For more than a decade one of the most planning-minded companies in this country had been Lockheed Aircraft Corpora-tion. From the very beginning, executives of this company, although they used to make frequent use of the term "master plan," have stressed that corporate programs are to be considered flexible, subject to continuous adjustment, revision, and review. "The master plan is not . . . a blueprint of fixed action steps over time which the Administrative Committee can pull out of a bottom desk drawer in the coming years to find the answers to a particular problem."[10] Certainly many other company execu-tives would agree with this statement.

5. ERRORS OF DEFINITION

All the obsessions just described are mirrored in certain com-mon definitions of planning. Any one of many common defini-tions could be used as a kind of summing up of the errors. "Optimal business planning is choosing, from alternative courses of action in the use of resources, those which will yield the highest possible discounted value of future net income flows," states one expert on business planning. A leading national or-ganization, with members from government and education as well as industry, uses a definition in which planning functions are specifically itemized—projecting future conditions, setting goals, devising and evaluating alternative courses of action, formulating measurement criteria for performance, and utilizing feedback

Imperial General Staff (New York, Doubleday & Company, Inc., 1957), p. 583.

10 L. Eugene Root (then a group vice-president of Lockheed) and George A. Steiner, "The Lockheed Aircraft Corporation Master Plan," in David W. Ewing (ed.), *Long-Range Planning for Management* (New York, Harper & Row, 1964), p. 372.

from performance in succeeding plans. There is only the faintest suggestion in these neat, logical, and antiseptic definitions of the messy, disorderly affairs of people! And there is little hint, in what many regard as the "technology" of planning, of the imprecise, fuzzy, judgment-based methods of the administrator. The "technology" is dominated by computable notions like project sequencing, expected value, mathematical programming, the simplex method, sensitivity analysis, and PERT—all important and of demonstrated utility, but on the material side of the ledger, not the human side.

Of course, there is a good historical reason for this mistaken emphasis in definition—Obsession Number Five. A great many of the men and women who have pioneered the "science" of planning have had backgrounds in operations research, economics, or similar specialties. It was only natural that they should, as I have heard more than one of them describe the effort, seek to "scientize" planning. What is surprising is that they were able to sell their definition to so many leaders and managers. The latter have impliedly accepted the nonhuman definition in the assignments they have given planning departments, in the standards of performance they have applied to planners, in the methods they have expected planners to use. I was talking one time to a senior executive in a large corporation who had just described to me some very impractical recommendations his planning experts had produced after long labors with economic projections, mathematical techniques, and a computer. When I wondered aloud that so much expertise could produce so little of practical value, he shrugged. "It's their way," he said. "They're like that. And it has its place, of course." *The planners have their place*, he was really saying, *but not in the real world*.

There is planning in the real world, of course—and it includes some superb planning. But it is overlooked because it so often lacks the paraphernalia of formal analyses and reports. During 1942 and 1943, General George C. Marshall did one of the world's great planning jobs when he helped to create long- and short-range programs for fighting the wars in Europe and the

Pacific. He used no decision trees, no quantitative models; if, in his innumerable meetings with theater commanders and Washington officials, he had detailed blueprints of the future complete with forecasts and alternative courses of action, he kept them well out of sight, for they are not mentioned in memoirs and historical accounts (although, of course, numerous studies were ordered by the Chief of Staff). What he did succeed in doing was to develop a kind of consensus concerning the general strategic approach that should be taken. Out of the welter of conflicting opinions advanced by all those who played important hands in Allied strategy, from Churchill and Stimson to MacArthur and King, he patiently sought to distill common notions about the military priorities between the European and Pacific wars, campaign strategies within each of those theaters, and effective command relationships. He was only partially successful—who *could* be completely successful in synthesizing the views of Churchill and MacArthur?—but he was successful enough to make effective action possible. In view of the almost endless number of alternatives that were possible, the very limited amount of resources available, and the many obstacles of enemy action, geography, and accident, his accomplishment must be ranked as a great example of planning.

At a less spectacular level, I know of a leading American oil company that owes much to the highly effective planning department it had some years ago. The planners in that department did not write up detailed programs for the operating departments, nor did they choose "optimum objectives" for different corporate functions. But they talked with the operating leaders and found what kinds of information were wanted and what kinds of assumptions were being made; they did their best to feed the relevant information to executives; and they organized "bull sessions" in which operating people could let their hair down and talk candidly with each other about questions of cooperation, coordination, and mutually satisfactory objectives. Out of all this began to emerge common notions about the corporate future and about the courses of action that were most desirable—notions that, it must be emphasized, became the bases *for executive decision*. Today this company has a more formal, more methodical planning activity, but it would not have come about but for the effective planning of a decade ago.

Ironically, however, the efforts of this oil company, as an example in business, and of General Marshall, as an example in government, would not come under the central focus of "planning" as so many of the experts describe it. Marshall's work might be called by them "persuasion" or "politics"; the oil company's, "pre-planning." To add to the irony, such experiences as that of the Kolyushchenko Construction Machinery Plant in Chelyabinsk, Russia, where in the first nine months of 1966 human endeavor in the plant was frustrated by sixteen major changes of program, *would* be called planning! (The ministry of construction and road building, which oversaw the plant, dictated three changes in the production plan, four in the capital investment program, six in the budget, and three in the finance program—all presumably because of a zealous desire to keep the plan technically efficient and up to date.[11]) For the original and follow-up programs for the Kolyushchenko plant, while poorly designed to elicit enthusiasm and cooperation, met the requirements of documentation, quantification, computer-tested inputs and outputs, economic logic, and industrial ideology!

It should be little wonder, then, that the ranks of planners have been subjected to an imbalance of talent. With the literature, job brochures, and other information emphasizing the technical, nonhuman definition, the kind of person interested in that approach has naturally been attracted to the field in large numbers. And with planning meetings, conventions, and educational programs emphasizing the nonhuman aspects, too, there has been little incentive for leaders and executive to join in and exchange experiences concerning how planning gets done in the "real world." We have a small case here of what C. P. Snow calls two *cultures*.

[11] S. Kamenitser and B. Milner, "Stimulation, Not Compulsion," *Liternaturnaya Gazeta* (U.S.S.R.), Feb. 1, 1967, p. 1.

The divergence has caused considerable difficulty in the planning movement.

The "Gutsy" Questions

Planning has gone wrong because it has been defined too often in terms of economic analysis, production capacity projections, distribution schedules, acquisition formulas, forecasts of demand, and other bloodless criteria—in these terms almost to the exclusion of the "people" aspects. As a result, there has been a tendency for the art and knowledge of planning to proceed in one direction while the art of management and leadership has proceeded in another. Neither planners nor skeptics of planning—neither the Lord Alan Brookes nor the Winston Churchills, to refer to the example cited—have benefited from this unfortunate trend. Planners have perhaps been the greater losers in the power play within the organizations, since they have generally operated at the second or lower levels of the hierarchy; but the skeptics have lost, too, for under them organizational performance has suffered when planning skills have been shunted.

Perhaps experts in planning have been making the same kinds of mistakes in their approach that many corporate analysts have been making in appraisals of company performance. Some telling comments on the latter came late in 1966 from George Olmsted, Jr., chairman of the S. D. Warren Company. Writing in his company's annual report for 1966, Olmsted observed:

Investors, security analysts, financial people, and others from time to time ask about the Warren Company. What's our productive capacity? How many tons will we ship? How do we figure depreciation? What profit will we make three years from next Michaelmas? And so on. All useful questions—no doubt.

But rarely, if ever, do they ask the one, real, "gutsy" $65 question —which is—what have you got for an organization? What sort of people are they? How do you recruit and train them? Who is going to run this business—and do the thinking for it—five years from now —ten years—twenty years?

This is the business. The rest is spinach.

In planning, a good part of "the business" is the tie-in between programs and people, between procedures on paper and operations in reality, between planned goals and the proven abilities and desires of the human organization. Unless these tie-ins are made carefully, thoughtfully, and realistically, all the numbers, ratios, projections, criteria, alternative programs, simulations, and schedules are of little value. They are, to use Olmsted's word, "spinach."

NOT HOUSES finely roofed or the stones of walls well-builded, nay nor canals and dockyards, make the city, but men able to use their opportunity.

—ALCAEUS

CHAPTER 4

The Disastrous Powers
of "Antiplanning"

IN THEORY, AT LEAST, it may seem relatively simple to develop a close tie-in between programs and people. To give planning greater currency, you simply make sure that the program is coined with two sides, a human side opposite the technical, material side. "Make sure your programs are adapted to the personal needs of your organization!" the authorities urge.

But in practice things are not nearly so easy. The practical problems of integrating programs and human behavior are, indeed, often baffling. And it is for this reason, too—not simply lack of interest and sophistication—that many managers have failed to make their plans part of the operational realities of their departments, divisions, agencies, or other organizations.

Probably the most universal difficult arises from people's *fears of planned change*. As indicated earlier, almost all ambitious plans are intended to produce new patterns of thought and action in the organization. However, as has been said innumerable times, people resist change—or, more accurately, they resist *being* changed by other people, e.g., planners. The problem is severe enough if the program stipulates new procedures for such employees as drill-press operators, salesmen, accountants, inspectors, soldiers, or whoever else may be concerned at the work level. Through their formal and informal unions, by means of such techniques as the slow-down and often simply though their ability to give or withhold psychological support from management, operators have considerable power to frustrate a leader's plan if they want to.

But the problem of introducing change can be even more severe if the program purports to alter the ways of "the Establishment." Here planners risk their necks as well as their aspirations. Leslie Hore-Belisha, Britain's Secretary of State for War from 1937 to 1939 who helped considerably to prepare his country for surviving the war with Germany, was a planner who knowingly accepted that risk and paid the penalty. Hore-Belisha tackled an ambitious long-range program for modernizing the British army (much of his program continued after he left office). However, carrying out his aims meant upsetting "the Establishment" in England during that period, in particular, the powerful Army Council, which was somewhat analogous to the Chiefs of Staff in the United States today. After Hore-Belisha had undertaken the initial steps to launch his program, he happened to have dinner one evening with a wise old hand at the British military game, Major General Sir Fabian Ware. During the conversation about the modernization program, the sixty-nine-year-old Ware told Hore-Belisha: "Nothing will happen at once, but you will find in the months ahead attacks on you from various quarters. There will be whispering in drawing-rooms and words will be dropped in influential ears. They will get you out."

Hore-Belisha asked, "How long will it take before they do get me out?" Major General Ware answered, "Eighteen months to two years." His prophecy turned out to be startlingly correct. Prime Minister Neville Chamberlain asked Hore-Belisha to resign in 1939, despite the strong support given the latter by Winston Churchill and others.[1]

This kind of experience—relatively quiet resistance from "the brass" at first, but with mounting attacks from a variety of quarters as time goes on, culminating in formal defeat of the planning leader—has repeated itself so many times in government and business that it might be called "Ware's Law." It is a law

[1] See R. J. Minney, *The Private Papers of Hore-Belisha* (Garden City, Doubleday & Company, Inc., 1961).

with loopholes—former Secretary of Defense Robert McNamara is perhaps the most publicized nullifier of it in the 1960's—and in remaining parts of this book we shall see how those loopholes can be greatly enlarged. Nevertheless, it is a law which practically every ambitious leader of change must learn to deal with.

There is another major hurdle to making programs operational. This one must be crossed regardless of how well Ware's Law is avoided, and more than once it has caused the downfall of a program that seemed to be in the clear as far as "the establishment" was concerned. This is the hurdle of *operating myopia*—the tendency of employees to absorb themselves in operating routines at the expense of planning efforts. A simple and interesting experiment with this tendency has been conducted. Let me describe it briefly.

A number of years ago four experts from System Development Corporation in California undertook a project involving ten groups of people.[2] The groups were given identical tasks to accomplish; the object for each group was to get the task done before the other groups did. Each group was given ample opportunity to organize, experiment with planning, and work out systems of cooperation. Moreover, it was made clear to each group that planning effort would be likely to pay handsome dividends in the efficiency contest. The result? Five of the groups made no attempt at all to organize and plan, three made abortive attempts and gave up, and only two groups succeeded (the latter were the ones that did best in the competition). "It is apparent," concluded the authors of the study, "that group planning, even under conditions that are highly favorable for its emergence, is inhibited by task pressure."

In the post-mortems on the competition, group members of the eight no-planning teams were asked about their failure to do more planning. A typical explanation was, "We were going so fast—you had to keep up with what you were doing."

Similar conclusions were reached by a leading authority, James

---

[2] Gerald H. Shure, Miles S. Rogers, Ida M. Larsen, and Jack Tassone, "Group Planning and Task Effectiveness," *Sociometry*, 1964, pp. 263–282.

G. March, after experiments with groups. The members were trained to perform a job requiring three kinds of activities— routine communication, intermediate planning, and general planning. The people were instructed to give equal attention to each type of activity. But once the pressure was on them to complete the task satisfactorily, they began putting more time on the routines at the expense of planning. When the work load was at a peak, planning virtually disappeared.[3]

Few executives who have attempted planning need to be convinced of the near-universality of these conclusions. In real life no less than in the group experiments, operating problems tend to drive out planning efforts. There are various reasons for this. One is that everyone has had more experience with operating problems, and most people feel more comfortable with them. By contrast, planning may seem like a foreign language. The table on p. 48 reproduces an interesting set of differences observed by a well-known consultant on industrial planning. Another reason is that reward systems generally favor the man who turns in a good *current* showing, whether measured in terms of profitability, sales volume, reduction of employee turnover, or some other way. Salary, bonus, and promotion rewards tend to be based on this month's, this season's, this year's performance—not contributions to goals three, four, or more years off. Still another reason, some executives tell me, is that there is so much job rotation in some organizations that a manager is unlikely to relate himself to results in a department that will not become apparent for several years.

Obviously no organization wants its managers to turn their backs on immediate problems. The question, therefore, is not an either-or one; it is not whether management should concentrate on planning *or* operations. Rather, the question is: How do we get managers and operators down the line to work on both operating *and* planning problems, in some appropriate balance?

[3] "Business Decision Making," *Industrial Research* (Carnegie Institute of Technology), Spring, 1959.

How Corporate Planning Differs from Operations

OPERATIONAL MANAGEMENT	CORPORATE PLANNING
1. Concerned with goals derived from established objectives.	1. *Concerned with the identification and evaluation of new objectives and strategies.*
2. Goals usually have been validated through extensive past experience.	2. *New objectives and strategies can be highly debatable; experience within the organization or in other companies may be minimal.*
3. Goals are reduced to specific sub-goals for functional units.	3. *Objectives usually are evaluated primarily for corporate significance.*
4. Managers tend to identify with functions or professions and to be preoccupied with means.	4. *Managers need a corporate point of view oriented to the environment.*
5. Managers obtain relatively prompt evidence of their performance against goals.	5. *Evidence of the merit of new objectives or strategies is often available only after several years.*
6. Incentives, formal and social, are tied to operating goals.	6. *Incentives are at best only loosely associated with planning.*
7. The "rules of the game" become well understood. Experienced individuals feel competent and secure.	7. *New fields of endeavor may be considered. Past experience may not provide competence in a "new game."*
8. The issues are immediate, concrete and familiar.	8. *Issues are abstract, deferrable (to some extent), and maybe unfamiliar.*

Reprinted by permission from Robert Mainer, *The Impact of Strategic Planning on Executive Behavior*, published in 1965 by Boston Safe Deposit and Trust Company.

If planning leaders successfully cross the hurdles of Ware's Law and operating myopia, they still have problems to surmount. There is the tendency toward *risk aversion*, prominent among all those managers who are asked to take the initiative in developing innovative programs of their own which will help the organization to achieve the broad aims conceived by leaders at the top. To plan is to reach into the unknown—to make estimates about what an organization can do and about what will happen. The unpredictable elements and variables begin mushrooming at an alarming rate when significant changes in goals and operations are contemplated. How can the manager be sure in his planning? He cannot. If he has a phobia about being wrong, if he is constitutionally and emotionally unfitted to work with question marks, planning will only add to his miseries, and all the talk in the world about the logic of and need for planning will not help.

Moreover, there is the risk of commitment. It is not every manager who welcomes the opportunity to clarify, in heated discussions with peers, subordinates, and bosses, what he thinks a department or division *should* organize to do. "We have enough troubles in this department getting along as we are," he says to himself, "without stirring up new animosities in debates over goals." Planning discussions, he fears, will create schisms; arguments over subjective judgments will add to the messiness of human relations. While day-to-day operating crises are bad enough, at least they are thrust on managers by events; no one can claim that the scars they create are self-inflicted.

An interesting observation bearing on this risk has been made by Roger A. Golde. His remarks are made with particular reference to small companies, but they are applicable to departments and divisions of larger organizations:

Even though most people don't talk about it, fear is a barrier to many kinds of activity. It is especially a road-block to planning, and it may be the biggest hurdle for most owner-managers.

Fear, for example, causes some owner-managers to feel that careful thought about the future of their companies will bring to light a host of troubles. "I've got enough worries without trying to cross bridges ahead of time," is a normal reaction.

Somehow it seems easier to live with vague apprehensions about a fuzzy future than it does with reasoned expectations. When the owner-manager has no clear description of the problems *and opportunities*, he tends to feel that his company can get by with token measures.[4]

The next major hurdle might be labeled the *one-world illusion*. No matter how sincere, intelligent, and "sold" on the planning idea, people in a sizable organization may resist a program because it appears to jeopardize their immediate interests. There is nothing "wrong" with this—unless human nature is wrong. What *is* wrong is for the planner to assume that his vantage point—his "world" of interests and ambitions—is the correct one for everyone else in the organization. For instance, a corporate program that is well designed to benefit the stockholders as a whole may be unpalatable to the heads of individual divisions because it forces them to gamble with new projects and investments. The division heads are not impressed by the argument that the corporation as a whole can afford such gambles. The planner at headquarters may figure, "One or two projects may not pay off, but enough of them will succeed to make our overall record very good." The division manager, on the other hand, may figure, "My gamble may be the one that fails—and where will that leave me? It will ruin our record."

The contrast between the planner's world and the operating executive's world may be particularly sharp in the so-called conglomerates (companies with divisions making completely different kinds of products, serving completely different markets, etc.). Norman Berg comments on the phenomenon as follows:

Managers at the *division* level are likely to have spent much of their working lives in their present or other divisions. Their "real world" is the people they see and work with every day, the products they manufacture, the physical facilities of the division, and the projects that are under way in the division. Customers and customer complaints are real; the products produced for them are tangible and

[4] "Breaking the Barriers to Small Business Planning," *Management Aids* Series No. 179 (Washington, D.C., Small Business Administration), September, 1965, p. 2.

are probably well understood. How well the product works and how efficiently it is produced are probably the result of innumerable personal challenges, successes, and failures. . . .

At the *corporate* level, in contrast, it is all too easy to feel that the real world consists of "the corporation" and those quantified abstractions which show how the corporation is doing with respect to the outside world—profit and loss statements, balance sheets, the market price of the stock, and so on. "*What does it mean in earnings per share?*" is often the all-important question with regard to division proposals or problems. The real world at the corporate level becomes the external and quantitative measure of corporate performance and health; divisions can all too easily be regarded as suppliers of financial statements which merely fit into the vast corporate totals.[5]

One more great obstacle to planning needs to be mentioned. An ambitious program for change typically forces some managers down the line to abandon or put aside projects which they have their hearts set on. Since they are naturally more interested in tending to their "babies" than someone else's, they find objections to the program. Some friends of mine at DuPont refer to this as the "*not-invented-here*" or NIH reaction. At DuPont, the term has to do mainly with a new product or process that one department is asked to develop and commercialize after another department has invented it. But NIH is a universal obstacle. In other companies it may explain resistance to new production methods or promotion concepts. In any organization it may explain efforts to reject planning.

A superb case in point is the introduction of radar for antisubmarine warfare (ASW) in World War II, for the "villain," from the planner's viewpoint, was no less than Admiral Ernest J. King, an exceptionally able and farsighted military leader. The chief "planner" in this episode was Secretary of War Henry L. Stimson. In 1942 he personally witnessed the great potential of airborne radar for ASW. (Radar had been first pioneered by the British, then taken over by Vannevar Bush's Office of Scientific

---

[5] "Strategic Planning in Conglomerate Companies," *Harvard Business Review*, May–June, 1965, p. 79.

Research and Development.) Stimson and such able members of his staff as Assistant Secretaries Harvey Bundy, John McCloy, and Robert Lovett—and with the support of General H. H. Arnold, General George Marshall, Edward Bowles, and others —began an intense campaign to sell the navy on using radar on its planes as a primary weapon in ASW.

Admiral King, the navy's commander-in-chief, strenuously resisted. He and the Navy Department experts were convinced, from experience in World War I and early experience in World War II, that the sovereign remedy against the submarine was the convoy system. ASW radar, they argued further, was inappropriate and difficult for navy fliers, in view of their unique operating problems. In addition, the navy was absorbed with so many urgent operating problems and with such severe material and personnel shortages that Admiral King and his aides were convinced it would be folly to divert limited energies and resources to a major innovation of unproved value.

After the navy rejected the proposal, Stimson, Arnold, Bowles, and others proposed to President Roosevelt that army planes be equipped with radar and undertake the ASW task. After lengthy debate in 1943 this proposal, too, fell by the wayside; the navy's objections were so strenuous that the idea was withdrawn for the sake of harmony and cooperation. And then a revealing thing happened: Admiral King, with the threat of departmental interference withdrawn, promptly launched efforts in the navy organization for the development of airborne ASW radar on navy planes![6] It thus seems evident that Stimson's charts and arguments had not seemed so impractical after all. The main trouble was that the idea had been invented outside the navy organization. Of course, other factors may have been present, too—the simple need for time to adjust to the concept, for instance—but NIH seems to have been the main one.

[6] See Elting E. Morison, *Turmoil and Tradition: A Study of the Life and Times of Henry L. Stimson* (Boston, Houghton Mifflin Company, 1960), pp. 561–577.

Avoiding Destruction

Forces like those described belong to what might be called the "world of antiplanning." In press reports in recent years we have heard about the mysterious new world of antimatter. Antimatter, it is said, is not apparent to the senses, but its existence can be demonstrated scientifically. It is known that when antimatter comes into contact with matter, the latter is exploded, completely destroyed as matter. Similarly, the world of antiplanning is not generally visible, audible, or touchable; it does not take the form of documents and charts, as officially sponsored programs do, nor do executives champion it in public statements, as they so often do in the case of planning. Yet the forces of anti-planning are fully capable of destroying planning when the two come sufficiently into collision.

This ever-present threat doubtless explains a large number of planning failures; also, it may well explain some of the tendencies to shun the human side of planning, as described in the preceding chapter. The technical, physical, quantitative recesses of planning afford a kind of escape, albeit a shortsighted one, from the collisions and shocks of human affairs and administration.

Obviously we do not want planning staffs and departments made over into personnel departments or organizational behavior research centers. Nor do we want vice-presidents in charge of planning or the titular leaders of new programs to turn away from the hard realities of finance, production, technological research, competition, product markets, and so forth. Yet if planning specialists and line executives in charge of planning neglect the social and political aspects that harbor antiplanning, how effective can planning be? Do members of planning departments want to be considered one-dimensional specialists who do not understand the art of getting things done through people? Are programs for change to be mere images without depth or substance, like Plato's shadows on the cave wall?

There are indeed proven ways of avoiding destruction from

antiplanning and of constructively linking programs with human operations. These ways will be examined in the next section. The ideal approach we seek is one that will make an organization (large or small and in whatever field) interested in and responsive to sound programs for change. It should be a flexible approach, one that can express planning-mindedness in a variety of forms for a variety of people and circumstances—not one that is patented for a special situation. It should be an approach for ordinary leaders in ordinary circumstances, as well as for exceptional leaders in exceptional circumstances.

This ideal of planning-mindedness as an *organizational* quality, not simply one great leader's, is vital to the philosophy we shall study in this book. If we restrict the possibilities of effective planning to the emergence of charismatic leaders, the temptation is overwhelming to sit back and wait for such a person to appear on scene, doing little or nothing until the time is ripe for him to take charge. Effective planning can be, should be, and, in the best cases, is a pervasive ability, one that may well have started in one place with one leader, but that ultimately flowers and matures in a whole human landscape of managers, supervisors, and specialists. In this form it is unformularized, it changes shape and style as the management team changes, it is adaptable to varying needs, it is diverse even to the point of sometimes seeming inconsistent.

For a down-to-earth illustration, take the case of Bell & Howell Company, Chicago's famous manufacturer of photographic, electronic, and other types of equipment. From the very beginning, the company's founding in 1907 by Donald J. Bell and Albert Howell, management has been planning-minded—well ahead, I would suspect, of most other corporate management groups in this respect. Yet planning has been approached in contrasting ways and manners in this company. And almost always the efforts seem to have been successful.

For instance, when Charles H. Percy was chief executive (he resigned in 1964 to run for governor of Illinois), planning for growth took the form principally of an acquisition strategy. In

1960 the company bought Consolidated Electrodynamics Corporation, an electronics-instrumentation firm with sales of about $44,000,000. And in 1962 it acquired Ditto, Inc., a leading manufacturer of office copying machines. After Peter G. Peterson became chief executive, however, the emphasis on acquisitions was dropped and the company turned to quite different routes to growth. It began pumping much more money into research and development of new products; it began arranging production and marketing alliances with other companies, such as Polaroid, DuPont, Xerox, and foreign concerns. These changes, made as a matter of changing moods and philosophies (not antitrust or financial restrictions), were carried out even though Peterson, as Percy's number-two man, had become intimately familiar with the earlier strategy.

The foregoing is not the only instance of Bell & Howell's rejection of formula. Another instance has to do with detail and execution. For years management has made and used formal, written plans. Even in 1957, long before most other companies had even considered the idea seriously, Percy was employing detailed, sixty-month programs. Notwithstanding the time and care that goes into these documents and the wealth of firsthand experience on which they are based, management will modify a plan sharply in mid-course, if it deems this wise, or even depart from the planned course of action. These departures represent "planning-mindedness," too, though of a more informal variety; they are not repudiations of planning.

What is more, management apparently does not feel bound to be consistent in its reliance on facts and figures. Percy, Peterson, and other top executives have made it a point to quantify goals and estimates with great care, wherever this could be done. When I first heard Percy speak on this point, a dozen years ago, he spoke proudly of how expense projections in company plans had been varying only slightly from actual incurred costs. Yet management is loath to think this way about all top-level decisions. Peterson, for instance, has stressed that some of the most important decisions have been based on "feel" for a situation and on the ability of executives "to imagine and do the unexpected." Once again, the latter do not really represent departures from or exceptions to planning, but a more intuitive, informal level of "thinking ahead" that management considers useful at certain times.

Bell & Howell's management is not even formula-bound in its marketing approaches, although in this area at least, the less sophisticated observer might think, consistency would be a virtue. Without doubt, planning is generally influenced by a strong marketing viewpoint in the company. Test marketing, marketing specialists, extensive market research—these and other approaches seem to be employed skillfully. Yet Peterson has spoken eloquently of the need to depart at times from a research orientation. He has expressed a strong belief in purposely going against the market tide on occasions and doing just the opposite of what market information seems to be telling the researchers. He feels this attitude is essential to marketing leadership.

THERE is nothing more difficult to take in hand, more perilous to conduct, or more uncertain in its success, than to take the lead in the introduction of a new order of things.

—NICOLO MACHIAVELLI

PART II:

Tailoring Programs to People

CHAPTER 5

The Needs of the Individual

THE HUMAN SIDE of planning, like the physical side, consists of different types of assets and resources. But these resources cannot be assessed by simple inspection, as physical assets can. They are too subtle for that.

The first subtlety is the seemingly bland question of what we mean by "people." For planning purposes, people are not simply "people." They are (1) individuals and (2) members of groups. Their needs in the two roles are different, and their impact on planning is different. This distinction, so easily stated, is of crucial significance to the planner. It is the beginning step, the underlying principle that must be understood if he seeks to proceed in his understanding and to progress in his sophistication.

In this chapter we will focus on the role of the individual in planning, saving for the ensuing chapter the question of group needs and influences.

Terms and Conditions

A member of an organization is first of all a person, only second an employee. When a plan affects his area of work, the first thing he wants to know is how it affects him. What bearing will it have on his desires for recognition, security, advancement, interesting work? If change in his behavior is called for, will he be able to do it himself, or will he have to *be* changed by someone else? Under the plan, can he remain true to his ideas about what is appropriate and fitting for him to do?

In organizations I know of in which planning is carried out successfully, managers in charge typically spend many hours talking with individuals about questions like these—explaining to them, listening to them, counseling them, analyzing their reactions, going back to ponder needed changes in strategy or tactics that will make the program more acceptable to individuals. It is not enough that the planned changes are justifiable in terms of what the *organization* needs for survival and growth (e.g., new product lines, lower costs, decentralized decision making, and so on). These latter effects must be explained, too, so that the individual can understand them, but their value in persuasion is more as rationalization for him than as primary motivation.

An old cliché in planning is that "planning must be sold to people." Often the inference is that *after* a new program is worked out in secret in the private offices of top executives, planning leaders should seek to make it palatable to employees. This is not the approach I want to describe here. The approach described here has to do with making a program *salable*—by so tailoring it and revising it *during* the architectural stage that it has the kind of content and substance that will command the support of key individuals.

Of course, there are some subtleties here. For instance, there is no neat distinction between salable content and methods of communication; how planning leaders go about discussing programs with people may well affect people's perceptions of the merits of the plan itself. To cite the most obvious kind of example, too often justifications for change are offered to individuals in memoranda, speeches, directives, and other impersonal types of communication. The trouble with such an approach is that it makes the implications of planning abstract. The individual does not change his ways in the abstract; he changes them in the offices, shops, territories, or other places where he works. So far as possible, his role in a new program should be demonstrated to him in these areas. If the plan calls, let us say, for a sales manager to report different information to a different person, an executive in charge can explain the new procedures to him in the offices and with the people who would be concerned and perhaps even go with the sales manager on a few trial runs. If the program calls for an engineer in charge of a new process to stay with it one stage further in the commercialization stage, the managers in charge should help him to visualize, in the laboratories and manufacturing areas where this new action would take place, what he would be doing, how, and with whom.

In all the history of planning there are probably few programs that were executed better in this respect than the United States agricultural extension service, pioneered early in the twentieth century by Seaman A. Knapp in the South and W. J. Spillman in the North and West (the Smith-Lever Act of 1914 was the legal heart of the service). The aim of this ambitious program was to achieve great gains in agricultural production by persuading farmers to use the improved techniques worked out in agricultural colleges and experiment stations. The method of achievement was to demonstrate to the farmer, right on his land or on neighboring land, how a technique worked. The demonstration was done by a "county agent." "This approach was settled on," writes Raymond W. Miller, "after long and disillusioning experience with bulletins, the lecture platform, the farmers' institute, government farms, the running of exhibition trains, and so on as alternative methods, all of which, it was sadly learned, accomplished very little."[1] The result of a demonstration was generally a doubling of the crop, whether it was cotton, corn, or legumes. In the early 1950's, the government of Nationalist China incorporated a similar concept in its program to increase agricultural output on Formosa; great gains, reports Miller, were again achieved.

Why is this simple technique of on-the-scene persuasion and demonstration so often overlooked when plans are made? Many

[1] "Our Economic Policy in Asia," *Harvard Business Review*, July, 1951, p. 66.

explanations might be given, but probably the most convincing one is simply that planners overestimate the logical appeal of their programs and underestimate the difficulty of making changes at the operating level. During hearings on the county agent system, Spillman once remarked: "I did not appreciate in my early days as an investigator the fact that when a farmer tried to put in application the recommendations I was making to him, he had a much bigger problem on his hands than I had in finding out what he ought to do."[2] With some changes in wording, this statement could be made into a general prescription for the planner in industry, education, or government: "I must appreciate that when a manager or other employee tries to put in application the changes I ask him to make, he has a much bigger problem on his hands than I have in finding out what he ought to do to achieve the planned goals."

Although this basic principle needs little elaboration, it would not be fitting to move on in our discussion without referring to the case of "Dashman Company."[3] This famous case illustrates a typical result of failure to tie a plan in with the needs of individuals who must carry it out. The company ("Dashman" is a fictional name for it) had over twenty plants in the United States when, late in 1940, the president brought in a man named Post to centralize the organization's purchasing procedures. This step was conceived as part of a plan to cope with increasing difficulties in obtaining raw materials needed in production. Right off, Post went to work on the problem by sending letters out to the executives who handled purchasing in the individual plants. The letter directed them to clear with him all purchase contracts over $10,000, and mentioned approval of the idea by the president and directors. Post explained in the letter: "I am sure you will understand that this step is necessary to coordinate the purchasing re-

[2] *Ibid.*

[3] A case copyrighted in 1947 by the President and Fellows of Harvard College. Reprinted in *Organizational Behavior and Administration*, by Lawrence, Bailey, Katz, Seiler, Orth, Clark, Barnes, and Turner (Homewood, Illinois, The Dorsey Press, Inc., and Richard D. Irwin, Inc., 1961), pp. 4–5.

quirements of the company in these times when we are facing increasing difficulty in securing essential supplies. This procedure should give us in the central office the information we need to see that each plant secures the optimum supply of materials. In this way the interests of each plant and of the company as a whole will best be served." Post did not visit personally with any of the men he wrote.

Replies to the letter arrived soon from executives in most of the plants. They would be glad to comply. But no evidence of compliance was received. No plant sent the head office a notice that a contract for more than $10,000 was being negotiated. However, executives from other departments at the corporate headquarters made frequent visits to the plants, and they reported that the plants were busy and that the usual routines were being followed.

In short, Post made the classic mistakes of assuming that (1) because the plan benefited the company in a logical manner, it would appeal to the individuals who must carry it out, and (2) the latter had no great problems of compliance which called for personal discussion at their places of work. For these mistakes the company suffered with the classic frustration: no implementation of the program.

Personal Counseling

Suppose in this case Post had visited with the plant executives before writing his directive. Would he then have been ready to proceed in the manner he did? Probably not. This answer brings us to another important principle to be observed in planning tactics. Time and again, when planning leaders have talked with those who must implement the programs, they find that simply conveying a clear understanding is not enough. More must be done than mere "hand-holding." The individual frequently has certain notions about himself and his role in the organization which make it far from evident, to him at least, that the planned change is sensible. He may believe the planned change demotes him. He may have friendships and political alliances that the change will upset. He may feel that the plan adds burdens on him which he is not prepared to accept. He may feel the plan requires changes in his supervision of others which are not in his interests or not in the interests of the organization as a whole. Whether or not he is right in fact is beside the point. As long as the individual *feels* this way, he is not likely to change his actions and thinking in the manner described no matter how patiently the program is explained and demonstrated to him. It becomes necessary actually to change the program, or introduce into it new measures that will meet the needs of the individuals affected, or make compromises. Sometimes—and this is the crucial point— even efforts like these will not be enough unless a planning leader can help the individual see his job and role in the organization in a new light. Such counseling was seen as a decisive factor in the planning undertaken by a large chain store organization.[4] In a subsequent chapter we will examine this counseling approach in more detail.

During meetings with planning executives over the years I have heard many unusual stories—some of them bordering on the bizarre, they were so extreme—about seemingly "irrational" individual reactions to new programs. There is apparently no end to the variety of frustration which planners can run into on this score. One of the more interesting documented cases concerns an economic organization in Scotland after World War II.[5] This organization—the Scottish Council—undertook a program to improve the capabilities and sophistication of electronics firms in Scotland. Leaders of this program, seeing that electronics companies in England, the United States, and other nations had learned new techniques that Scottish companies had not, realized that a disastrous gap might be widened between the know-how of the Scottish companies and their competitors on the world market.

---

[4] See Paul R. Lawrence, *The Changing of Organizational Behavior Patterns* (Boston, Harvard Business School Division of Research, 1958).

[5] See the authoritative study by Tom Burns and G. M. Stalker, *The Management of Innovation* (London, Social Science Paperbacks, in association with Tavistock Publications Ltd., 1961).

To cope with this threat, the Scottish Council worked out a scheme that seemed then—and does still in retrospect—eminently reasonable and practical. A contract would be set up with an electronics company, either at its own initiative or at the initiative of the Scottish Council. The company would then learn of electronics research facilities available by arrangement to the council, and a representative of the company would be invited to visit them. After the company's management had chosen an area of technology in which it was especially interested, it would assign some of its engineers to work on a development contract with experts in the council laboratories. After these engineers had mastered the techniques required for the contract, they would return to the company, where in the meantime a suitable laboratory would have been prepared. Thus, the company would pick up knowledge and skills which would help it to acquire new business in an important area of its choosing. It preserved its autonomy and independence; it preserved its right to develop at its own pace and in the sectors that interested it; it was forced to take no unreasonable risks or financial commitments. The scheme was a kind of pump-priming operation designed by a business-sponsored association to help local business survive.

Yet the plan failed. Most of the Scottish firms failed to realize the goals of the program. "In half of the cases, company laboratory groups which had been set up were disbanded or disrupted by the resignation of their leaders," Burns and Stalker report. "Others were converted into test departments, 'trouble-shooting' teams, or production departments."

Why did this sensible system fail—this unselfish program to help local business prosper in a changing world? A careful investigation was made to determine the answer. The trouble, it was learned, was that the internal politics of the Scottish companies was threatened. To the employees in these companies, a new laboratory group in a company meant a new power group, a new elite. What was, to the Scottish Council, the most compelling argument for such a group—pervasive technological change— became, for managers in many of the companies, the most damaging argument *against* it; that is, the very urgency of the need for innovation suggested it would upset existing political relationships, alliances, and balances of power in a company. Concerns and possibilities like these were far more real, important, and absorbing to an individual manager with ambitions for control and status than were world trends in electronics technology.

Common Symptoms

Later in this book we shall see how some planning leaders have coped successfully with problems like the foregoing. It must be admitted now, however, that so far as we know, no universal formula for solving these tactical problems exists; since the people involved are not interchangeable, neither are the correct methods of approach. (For instance, had the Scottish Council situation been replicated in Japan, the plan might have worked admirably.) However, we can detect certain common symptoms of failure to take the human aspects properly into account.

"Polite talk" accompanied by inaction and plausible-sounding excuses for inaction is one such symptom. In the Dashman case, Post received prompt answers like these from executives in the plants: "Your recent communication . . . has been received. This suggestion seems a most practical one. We want to assure you that you can count on our cooperation." I have often heard executives suggest that if a new program does not stir up some cries for problem-solving help from headquarters, it does not "smell right." A social machine does not change speed without a little gear-clashing.

A less obvious symptom is preoccupation with personal fault-finding. If an individual finds he is not prepared to go along with a program for change especially in the sense of not feeling ready to work with other people in the new ways that are necessary, he is likely to take his frustrations out on them. He faults them for being untactful, unfair, stupid, incapable, although perhaps agreeing that the new program itself is perfectly reasonable. This reaction was noticeable in the Scottish Council case, and certainly many managers in American companies are familiar with it. Of course, it *may* be that the complaints are in fact justified; the individual may indeed be encountering more than a normal share of incompetence and ill will. Nevertheless, a manager with a good "feel" for people's reactions will take a pattern of such fault-finding as a warning flag: organizational difficulties created by misplanning tend to be converted into complaints against other employees.

The importance of subtleties like the foregoing has something to do, I am sure, with the fact that successful executives are prone to depart from the textbook description of their roles. So often one sees and hears of them breaking away from the neat, logical formalities of planning, controlling, and evaluating which occupy so many textbooks. The executives may appear to be "wasting" time by getting involved in an operating matter that seemingly could be left to a subordinate, or they may appear to be paying more attention to the grapevine than to dollars-and-cents priorities. But the excursions are not really irrelevant to planning. They are probes beneath the cutaneous layer of allegation and rationalization, efforts to find human drives and resistances which individuals have no satisfactory way of reporting in planning documents.

My INTEREST is in the future because I am going to spend the rest of my life there.

—C. F. KETTERING

CHAPTER 6

The Invisible Hand of the Informal Group

ALTHOUGH THE ROLE and influence of informal groups of employees are rarely mentioned in the literature on planning, they are of decisive importance. For one thing, the informal group plays a vital part in achieving organizational goals. For another, it influences the behavior of individuals, thus having a fateful bearing on the subject discussed in the previous chapter. Both of these roles will be discussed presently.

The informal group is so called because it is usually seen on no organizational chart and generally has no legal or formal membership requirements. It is made up of people who, for one reason or another, relate to each other in the work to be done. It may consist of employees of a certain age in an organization or perhaps employees possessing a certain skill or aptitude. Often the group is formed because of the way the work is done or where it is done. For instance, the members of an informal group may be the drill-press operators in a production line, the maintenance men in a plant, the "missionary" salesmen in a territory as opposed to the "account maintenance" salesmen, the managers and their assistants in the Toledo office, the copywriters in an advertising firm, or the yeomen in a navy unit. In some cases, the membership of an informal group may be identical with that of a formal group, too; for instance, the union members in a plant having both unionized and nonunionized employees may comprise both a formal and informal group. When participating in a union function, they act as a formal group; but when showing more kindness to each other than to nonunion employees, they act as an informal group.

Informal groups have amazing abilities to resist pressure and manipulation from outside planners. At the outset of the United States military occupation of Japan, for instance, a determined effort was made to destroy the Zaibatsu system—the traditional role of the family in the control of economic enterprises in Japan. But the family group relationships that underlay the system could not be destroyed, nor could the system's instinctive appeal to other groups in Japanese industry. Even though the Zaibatsu system was legally and formally eliminated for a few years, it had to be restored in order to speed the rebuilding of the Japanese economy. On the other hand, numerous other aspects and functions of Japanese society which were not sustained by group feelings were changed very successfully by the occupation.

Impact on Planned Organizational Change

The first thing a planning leader must appreciate about the informal group is that it rarely reacts in a completely neutral way to a program. For all practical purposes, it will exert either a plus or a minus effect. Its manner of reaction depends in no small part on whether the plan is conceived in terms that make sense to it. As Kurt Lewin once said in speaking of an educator's ability to mold the behavior of a student group, a strong "we feeling" must be created between the two.

It may be refreshing to turn to a famous historical example at this point (the informal group, like so many other factors discussed in this book, has been affecting plans and planners for hundreds of years). In 1588, King Philip II of Spain planned the invasion of England by his Armada. The informal group on this historical occasion was the Catholic population of England (admittedly a larger body than we usually think of in discussions of group behavior). In his calculations, King Philip counted on English Catholics to rise against Queen Elizabeth and her minister, Lord Burghley, when his plan went into operation. The plan consisted of two major steps: first, achieving control of the English Channel, this to be done by the Armada, and, second, the ferrying of the Spanish army, commanded by the Duke of Parma in the Netherlands, across the Channel to English shores. Perhaps because he was obsessed with the military might of his army and navy, Philip announced his goal as the deposing of Queen Elizabeth. This had little appeal to English Catholics, who generally preferred to suffer persecution from fellow Englishmen than from a Spanish Infanta. Hence they offered no support when the Armada approached, most Catholics joining vigorously in the defense of the realm. In reacting in this way, they apparently were influenced by a kind of group consensus about what was proper to do; the "we feeling" excluded Philip even though he was a fellow Catholic.

Suppose Philip had conceived of his plan in terms that would have appealed to the Catholic group. What would have happened then? He might well have obtained its active help, with all that would have meant for his chances of success. Two leading historians, Sir Charles Petrie and T. Maynard, believe that Philip's plan would have had this effect if the goal had been conceived of as restoring religion in England, with no intention of overthrowing English political rule.[1] Such a goal would have put Philip's relationship with English Catholics in a different light. Indeed, perhaps many Catholic merchants frankly hoped for some such development when, prior to the invasion, they sold cannon, powder, and other supplies to Spain.

No such mistake in overlooking group influence was made by those who planned the United States occupation of Japan after World War II (although they did misjudge the strength of the Zaibatsu system, as we have seen). One of the goals that General MacArthur and the State Department held uppermost was a

[1] See Sir Charles Petrie. *Philip II of Spain* (New York, W. W. Norton & Company, Inc., 1963). The author relies partly on T. Maynard's study, *Queen Elizabeth*.

stable, conservative, representative Japanese government that could resist the blandishments of Stalinist Communism. One large and important group that therefore received much attention was Japanese farmers. The occupation plan administered by Mac-Arthur included healthy doses of land reform to give the once downtrodden peasantry a strong stake in the new system. Ever since then the farm group in Japan has provided consistent support for conservative political parties, more than counteracting leftist elements in the cities.

Unfortunately, when goals and timetables for a new program are being prepared, the actions of informal groups are not always so predictable as in England in 1588 and Japan in 1946. This leads us to a second principle that the planning leader must observe: a potent group may be catalyzed by the program itself. A group that previously has been largely dormant and inactive may "come alive." This principle has been demonstrated repeatedly during the past two decades as companies, schools, public agencies, and nonprofit institutions have sought to install computer information systems, procedures of quantitative analysis, and other innovations. Resistance has come from "oldsters"—but not all senior people, just those who combined seniority with certain other characteristics (often personality traits or aptitude weaknesses). *Some* oldtimers, in fact, have been promoters of the new tools and concepts. The point is that the informal group that does coalesce and become a factor in progress may have had no precedent; it is brought into being by a combination of circumstances, an often subtle and chemical-like reaction of elements in the plan, the environment, and the people affected. The mysteries in this process may be fully as great as in forecasting market demand for a new product or public reaction to a new service program.

A third principle is that the informal group generally has a conservative influence on planning. Far more often than not, it exerts a braking effect on a program for change rather than an accelerating effect. The explanation need not concern us here, although obviously it is connected with the tendency of group members to form relationships and to want to protect those relationships against outsiders' intrusions. The phenomenon is a familiar one in large conglomerate corporations, among other organizations. A never ending struggle is often seen between allegedly "unrealistic" planners in corporate headquarters and allegedly "myopic" managers of the various operating divisions. As pointed out previously, to the men at headquarters (and to the stockholders) it may seem eminently sensible to ask all divisions to invest in fairly risky projects; now and then one will fail, but the failures will be more than offset by the successes, at least in the long run. To the division head and his top assistants, however, a good corporate-wide batting average is less compelling. Suppose *their* division is the one that strikes out? For them there is little warmth in the knowledge that the corporate dividend was increased as they go looking for jobs in other companies. Much the same can sometimes be said about the departments within divisions, in the case of divisional planning. The production department, the research group, the marketing department, the purchasing branch—the members of each of them tend to collaborate to assure that their groups "stay in business" without unreasonable risk. If the odds are different for them than for the division as a whole, who can blame them when they give halfhearted support to a program that is logical only from the planning leader's standpoint?

Finally, the significance of a program for an informal group depends on whether or not the program goals are pertinent to the basis of attraction of the group. Why does a labor union seem to be able to exert much stronger discipline over its members in dealings with management than in political action? One reason is that a person joins a union mainly to protect his job and improve working conditions, hence in those matters the union means far more to him than in politics. In politics he may be more susceptible to suggestion from, say, a political club or civic group, which he has joined because of its political interests. Similarly, an informal group of technical maintenance men in a plant might be eagerly concerned about a modernization program for the equipment but indifferent to a revolutionary marketing plan, even though the latter has just as great long-range significance for their security in the company as the former does.

Influence on the Individual

The actions and attitudes of an individual are almost always a reflection at least in part of the groups to which he belongs. Is he aggressive? Is he confident? Is he cooperative? The answers to these and many other questions depend on what cliques, clusters, and informal unions he associates with. Consequently, his reactions to a planned change are likely to be influenced by the general posture and attitudes of the group. This relationship can be and often is of enormous importance.

Specifically, plans to increase productivity, technical know-how, or skills are likely to be influenced by group-individual relationships. Logically, such a plan appeals to the self-interest of many individuals. If it is an incentive plan for piece-rate workers, it means (if it is fair) that those who apply themselves diligently to the job can increase their take-home pay. Yet if an operator exceeds some unwritten group rule as to how much work should be done, he runs the risk of being considered disloyal. Again, if a plan calls for scientists to spend more time on manufacturing problems with new processes, it should mean financial benefits for the individual scientist and perhaps a "leg up" on the management side, if he wants it. Yet that may mean working more regular hours, and if there is an unwritten rule among scientists that it is inappropriate for their breed to be subjected to the "nine-to-five rat race," the individual may find his friendships with colleagues strained if he begins arriving punctually at the plant every morning.

A person's planning horizons are also likely to be influenced by the groups to which he belongs. Psychologists have found that the time horizons of children vary considerably depending on the stability, comfort, security, and other aspects of their family environment. Similarly, the time perspective of a manager is influenced by the situation of the group in which he works. People in certain industries are notoriously preoccupied with the present, while men and women in others have long been known to project years ahead into the future; for instance, contrast the women's apparel or the toy industries with timber-growing or airline transportation. Such differences in group temporal perspective, quite apart from the economic or technical causes of the differences, cannot fail to affect individual habits and norms. Equally significant, within the same company there may be great variations in temporal horizon due to differences in function and perhaps to differences in average age or background. A few years ago I heard a top planner with a leading auto manufacturer describe the lengths of planning periods in different departments of his company. Financial executives had plans extending twice or more as far into the future as did marketing managers. Clearly, the temporal horizon a planner in this company could expect of a given individual depended heavily on which group the individual was associated with.

This is a good place to emphasize that the informal group by no means is always a restricting influence on the individual. (The examples used here and elsewhere in the literature may suggest that.) The group may have just the opposite kind of influence: it may help the individual to break out of the ruts of the past. A good many of us could no doubt testify to this from personal experience, describing how belonging to a new group in the military service or a business corporation—or perhaps even a new family association—educated us to demand more of ourselves than in the past. As the French psychologist, Paul Fraisse, once pointed out: "In order to become better men, we must often burst our present limits, and then our social group lends us irreplaceable aid in offering us new possibilities, and with them new horizons, not only for ourselves, but for all mankind."[2]

From a planning standpoint, one of the most significant influences of the group on the individual has to do with learning and

---

[2] "The Worker's Adaptation to Time," *Bulletin du Centre d'Etudes et Recherches Psychotechniques*, April–September 1958.

experimentation. The small informal group with which he works is a kind of learning laboratory. When he begins to have new feelings toward the organization, its management, or its programs —a changed feeling of loyalty, let us say, or a different view of the importance of certain work—it is in the group that he usually begins testing his changed feelings, deciding whether or not they make sense, wondering whether or not to talk about them even more or perhaps not at all. Two behavioral scientists have noted: "The small group is a strategic focus for practical, applied change programs as well as for research because it transforms social abstractions, such as culture, values, and tradition, into concrete, observable, and to some degree controllable interpersonal events. The small group setting is where reality testing, on the one hand, and emotional contagion, on the other, actually take place."[3]

The group also influences a member's sense of values. This is important to the planner because his programs frequently rest on notions about what is fair, appropriate, and responsible to ask a person to do. How important is money-making as compared, say, to performing a public service? How important is it to keep loyal employees secure in their jobs at the expense, say, of achieving a planned goal a little faster or more dramatically? Is it very important for the organization to be a leader in research, new knowledge, original methods and concepts? The way an employee answers such questions is influenced by the feelings of his close associates. A person who joined the staff of *The New York Times* would find himself being influenced to value intelligent, accurate, objective reporting of the news as something "good" for its own sake, whereas in some other publications his associates would be encouraging him to favor sensationalism and provocativeness at any price. Obviously, such pressures could be important factors for or against planning, depending on how much the program is consistent or inconsistent with them.[4]

[3] Abraham Zaleznik and David Moment, *The Dynamics of Interpersonal Behavior* (New York, John Wiley & Sons, Inc., 1964), p. 454.
[4] For this and other examples of the influence of values on organizational behavior, see William D. Guth and Renato Tagiuri, "Personal Values and Corporate Strategies," *Harvard Business Review,* September–October, 1965.

The invisible hand of the informal group is an awesome thing in planning. Its impact is being documented with increasing frequency as social scientists study organization, and historians of the future will probably pay far more attention to it as an explanation of events. As for the past, one can only speculate about how often it was the informal group, rather than unusual strengths or weaknesses in leadership, which made events come out as they did. Certainly we can be confident that such cases, were they known, would be endlessly varied, ranging from wandering, mixed-up business companies that suddenly sprang to life in the pursuit of rather ordinary goals, to powerful, seemingly potent public agencies that accomplished nothing despite dramatic programs and an atmosphere of initial excitement. How often should the explanation have been the informal group rather than "charismatic leadership"? How often should the blame on "bureaucracy" have been shifted to the informal group?

Actions and Responses

Successful planners can be seen paying daily respect to group power. For one thing, they do a lot of listening. An executive involved in a program to reorganize a company's structure is seen getting a group of supervisors around a table. He asks them one by one to give their opinions on how the plan is working. He is not trying to manipulate this particular informal group so much as to sound it out; when the members are together, giving each other mutual support, they are more likely to be candid about any criticisms or complaints they feel. One student of cases of organizational change finds this information-gathering step a continually reappearing element in successful efforts to change, and he believes it has values other than diagnosis—evidence to subordinates that planners are willing to change, for instance, and evidence of interest in solutions proposed by people at the operating levels.[5]

[5] See Larry E. Greiner, "Patterns of Organizational Change," *Harvard Business Review*, May–June, 1967, p. 119. This article was part of a larger

Keeping free and open communication within a group, between it and other groups, and between any group and the executives to whom it reports also helps the organization in an organic way. Behavioral scientists find that a pathological group—that is, one that has trouble in decision-making, coordinating, or effecting desired changes in its behavior—typically is crippled by communication difficulties among its members. Conversely, healthy groups—that is, ones that seem to change naturally and easily as needs and objectives change—typically have adequate communication among members. The more the planner can work to encourage the latter, therefore, the greater his advantage in getting action. Of course, planning itself is a superb vehicle for opening up communication. Especially if the plan deals with the problems and aspirations employees already possess (rather than imposing on them problems or objectives which seem remote or abstract), the executive in charge can use it to bring group members together and get them talking.

Irwin T. Sanders describes a plan in which he was involved to further racial integration in New York City schools.[6] A school was purposely placed in an area populated by low-income Negroes, low-income Puerto Ricans, and high-income whites. Integration was expected. A number of the white families were agitated, and they opposed the program. Recognizing the importance of keeping communication lines open and of encouraging people to examine questions for themselves, social workers helped parents to hold tea parties and meetings for discussion of the school question. The social workers brought principals and schoolteachers to the meetings. Many questions and arguments were discussed. Subsequently, about 50 percent of the area's white children came into the school. Without the meetings, Sanders is convinced, the results would not have been nearly so successful.

In this instance of civic planning, the plan leaders took official action to open communication lines. In perhaps the majority of instances with which most of us are familiar, however, the man-

---

study by Greiner, Louis B. Barnes, and D. Paul Leitch for the Harvard Business School Division of Research.

[6] Morris (ed.), *op. cit.*, p. 123.

agers step out of their official roles—or, at least, their official roles at described in textbooks—to carry out dialogues with informal groups. A vice-president of a division will become involved in a problem that worries foremen in the plant; according to "the book," he should be delegating such matters to managers at lower levels, but the action gives him opportunities to listen personally to what foremen are thinking and to sense what their attitudes are. That information is extremely important to him as a policy-maker and planner. Military leaders have been known to do much the same thing; well-known examples are Generals Eisenhower and Patton during World War II.

The principles we have considered in this chapter must be qualified in two ways. First, planning leaders can sometimes change the informal groups with which they deal so that the people will support a preconceived plan, instead of vice versa. For instance, the atmosphere in which the group works may be changed, or the problems with which it deals, or the people who compose it. Second, there *are* times when a dictatorial leader can put an ambitious plan into action without paying much attention to the role of groups. This can happen in times of crisis when the craving for strong direction is so great that it outweighs the usual interests—the "do-anything-so-long-as-you-do-something" mood that often arises during wars and natural disasters. It can also happen when, for one reason or another, informal groups have not been able to form well in an organization.

DON'T BE afraid to take a big step if one is indicated. You can't cross a chasm in two small jumps.

—DAVID LLOYD GEORGE

The Art of Relating Goals to People

PLANNING CONSISTS of two major phases, the strategic or goal-setting phase and the implementational or "carrying-out" phase. In *each* of these phases it is crucial to consider the role of individuals and groups in the organization, as discussed earlier.

Unfortunately, there seems to be a tendency among planners to defer the human aspects to the second phase. It is apparently assumed that if the goals are "right" in economic or other material terms, then surely the organization can be manipulated to pursue these goals vigorously and achieve them on schedule, providing that management combines the carrot and stick properly. In actuality, this is not the case. Many plans are doomed from the start, no matter how skillfully individuals and groups are handled in the implementation, because the goals chosen are not realistic for the people involved.

Some organizations may be exempt from this concern because they have leaders capable of inspiring followers in almost any direction they choose. But such exceptions occur more rarely than we like to think. As a matter of fact, perhaps the greatest villain in strategic planning is the leadership group that is almost-but-not-quite charismatic. Overconfident of its abilities to manage and inspire—or perhaps overenthusiastic in its sense of mission—it picks objectives that are beyond or foreign to the abilities of those who must do the day-to-day work.

But errors in the choice of goals are not due alone to failings in leaders' self-judgments. They are also due frequently to failings of method. As emphasized in an earlier chapter, there has been a tendency to start formulating goals in terms of ideals, markets, public needs, or other considerations *external* to the organization and only secondarily (or possibly as an afterthought) in terms of what the human organization is capable of achieving. Theoretically the human side can receive adequate consideration when this approach is taken. In practice, however, things do not work out that way much of the time. When the external judgments come first, they tend to dominate the planner's thinking, to become a kind of preoccupation, making it difficult for him to see the human side realistically.

For an analogy, consider the difficulty one has with a drawing that can be viewed in two ways. A well-known example is a sketch that simultaneously portrays the faces both of an old woman with a shawl and a pretty young woman. But usually the viewer sees one *or* the other, not both. One stands out if the eye catches one set of lines first, the other if another set of lines is seen first. Once a person gets one version of the drawing in mind, he has great trouble changing his mental gears and seeing the other version. Judging from the planning experiences with which I am familiar, much the same difficulty occurs when leaders become enthusiastic about the opportunities presented by an external trend or condition, *then* ask themselves if their organizations would be able to exploit the opportunities. Warning messages about the latter ability may be perfectly clear but not seen.

One of the most important new trends in planning seems to be the rise of a new approach to goal-setting. This new approach is basically "inner directed" rather than "other directed." It means beginning with assessments of internal strengths, talents, and abilities, and only then turning to the external environment and asking where the best opportunities lie for exploiting these abilities. This approach is coming to be called the "inside-out" approach to strategic planning.[1] (This label contrasts it with the "outside-in" approach of beginning with the analysis of external trends and

[1] See the author's book, *The Practice of Planning* (New York, Harper & Row, 1968), Chapter 5.

needs and then seeing if the organization can be prepared to meet them.)

Of course, the inside-out approach means running just the opposite risk of the one just described—namely, the risk that internal assessments will overshadow appraisals of markets and industry conditions. But judging from the evidence thus far, that risk is slighter than the risk of outside-in planning. One reason is that an empirical marketing judgment appears to be built into judgments of organization talents and abilities. If experience shows that the organization seems to have a great ability to innovate and pioneer with new products and services, that conclusion will be based on past successes in innovation; those successes would not have happened if the buying public had not liked the new products. Again, if the record shows that the organization is highly "efficiency minded" and has an unusual ability to concentrate on repetitive production runs of specialized products (Volkswagen during the long postwar period of manufacturing the unchanging "beetle" design, for instance), that conclusion will be based on successes with such production in the past; those successes were made possible by market acceptance.

In industry there is ample evidence that the company that can correctly assess an unusual set of organization talents can actually create growth opportunities for itself—even in industries supposedly overrun by numerous competitors and possessing, in the view of market forecasters, no future at all for expansion.[2] Such a company finds the key to success not in market appraisals but in self-appraisals—not in understanding the outside world but in understanding the special abilities of its own managers and workers.

Does inner-directedness, with its emphasis on the human side, mean a flaunting of the marketing viewpoint? Not really. Consider the case of Herman Miller, Inc., a leading furniture designer located in Zeeland, Michigan. This company works in an inside-out way on new product decisions; a designer gets an idea for a new piece of furniture, works on it and discusses it with other

[2] *Ibid.*, pp. 53–56.

designers, and not until the idea has got out of the concept stage do marketing managers get in on the act and ask about salability and pricing. Moreover, if there is a division of opinion between designers and the sales group, the designer generally wins; his judgment of marketability is considered a better bet than the market researcher's or the salesman's. Thus, to use *Business Week*'s words, the company mows down "many a sacred cow of marketing."[3] Actually, however, Herman Miller's is not an anti-marketing approach. For time after time in the past, the designer here has been right about the potential appeal of a new design; so long as management continues to recruit, train, and work with designers as it has done in the past, it can expect them to continue to be right, for clearly this organization has worked out a unique "formula" for using design talent to *create* new markets. Accordingly, when management "gambles" on its designers' judgment about a new design, it is not really taking a long chance on the market; it is taking a calculated risk with the odds well in its favor.

Sound, thoughtful inside-out planning has worked for organizations of all kinds and sizes in industry, education, the health and welfare field, and other areas. Although procedures and styles of inside-out naturally vary, certain steps are basic to the approach in almost any situation:

1. Analyze the talents and abilities of people in the organization, as well as its material resources, to see if certain types of effort and expenditure have been paying off especially well.

2. Consider the possibilities of beefing up the key abilities or supplementing them so that they will be more effective still in the future. Seek to visualize the strength the organization could have if, through planning, all decisions and actions (from hiring and training to the organization and assignment of work) served to reinforce these core abilities.

3. Examine the goals that would then be within reach of the organization. These might be more ambitious goals in present fields of work—or perhaps objectives in entirely different fields.

4. Check the marketing picture (or other environment of the

[3] December 19, 1964, p. 61.

organization) carefully to see if there are unusual obstacles or "no-go" signs affecting the feasibility of these goals. Inside-out planning by no means calls for overlooking markets, public needs, or other external conditions. The latter are essential check points. They may indicate that certain goals are impractical or undesirable no matter how uniquely qualified the organization is to achieve them. For instance, an otherwise promising marketing goal may wisely be discarded because of expected technological developments that will revolutionize demand trends; or there may be an antitrust problem or a hopeless bottleneck in the supply of some critical item needed for production.

5. If no goal or set of goals clearly emerges as highly desirable the first time through steps one to four, go through the procedure again. Usually, in fact, the inside-out process is circular in nature, going on more or less continuously in planning leaders' minds.

Rejecting the Impossible Dream

The inner-directed, inside-out approach to goal-setting has been, and probably always will be, nurtured better in industrial settings than in government. Business leaders as a whole are more pragmatic, better-trained economically, and less missionary-minded than political leaders. Government may have its shrewd politicians, but the needs it must meet are urgent and desperate, and the fires of idealism are continually being fanned by new winds. There are more men of La Mancha ready to fight for "impossible dreams"—and just often enough to keep their hopes alive, one succeeds.

Nevertheless, one can see in government planning a distinct tendency to take more realistic notice of what the people affected are willing and able to do—even if this means making unpleasant compromises with the ideals planners would like to strive for. And this is being done in some of the areas in which, because of urgent and dire needs, the discipline of inside-out planning is hardest to accept. One such example seems to be the Basic Development Plan recently worked out for the Calcutta (India) Metropolitan District, 1966–1986. This is an imaginative program for one million people in desperate living conditions. Most of them are tenants of slum landlords. But the plan does not contemplate slum clearance. Instead it looks to government purchases of the land followed by reselling of parcels to the present tenants. The terms of sale call for long deferred payments. The government is to install sanitary facilities and deepen the wells to produce pure water, but further improvements are left to the resident owners. The planners believe the owners will make such improvements as a sense of community solidarity deepens and confidence in the fact of ownership grows. One of the planners reportedly confided once that he *could* have laid out instead an entire and perfect model of slum clearance for the twenty-year period, but he did not do so because he realized that such an idealistic plan would only gather dust. He knew that goals had to be tailored to the psychology of the people, else they were not valid. Achievement would be slower this way—but more sure.

Another interesting application of the inner-directed philosophy occurred some years ago in Iran. This one, too, involved a team of United States experts working with nationals, and while the project was frustrated at the last moment, the thinking that went into it will surely become a precedent for later ventures of this type. Beginning in the late 1950's, a highly skilled, professional planning team drew up for Iran—an ancient civilization with fine economic potential, an invigorating climate, an area three times the size of France, and with 45,000 villages and no shortage of arable land—a five-year program of economic growth to begin in 1962.[4] The program contained a series of steps for increasing the national output at a rate of 6 percent per year, improving the living standards of rural people and improving the distribution of income. Very wisely the planners in Tehran tailored the overall

[4] An authoritative and highly readable report of this experience is contained in George B. Baldwin's book, *Planning and Development in Iran* (Baltimore, The Johns Hopkins Press, 1967). The author was a member of the Harvard advisory group that assisted the Iranians. A similar advisory arrangement had been notably successful in Pakistan.

objectives as well as the objectives of the smaller component programs to their best judgments of what the people would support. For instance, although they recognized that land reform would eventually be necessary (Iran had an outmoded landlord-tenant system), they appreciated that the country was not ready yet for massive reforms; intermediate steps were necessary first. Accordingly they subordinated idealized changes in the land tenure system to the goal of raising production, particularly agricultural production. Again their program called for the government to concentrate its efforts on regions in which productivity and income were already highest, neglecting for the time being some large regions in which economic conditions were worst. The planners recognized that to spread the government's effort over all regions would dilute it too much and make accomplishment anywhere unlikely. This constraint resulted from limited human resources (including interest and understanding of progress as well as talent) and great demands for coordination, cooperation, banking, irrigation, and other efforts. For motivating people to carry out the programs, the planners employed a judicious combination of informational campaigns, technical assistance, demonstration plots, financial aid, and training programs.

Just as this workable plan was about to go into operation, however, the Shah and a crusading Minister of Agriculture derailed it. They committed the government's limited resources for change to a dramatic land-reform program instead. They did this because by chance there occurred in 1962 a temporary absence of landlord representation in the parliament, so that the country was in effect being ruled by decree for a period. The crusading Minister of Agriculture convinced the Shah, who was sympathetic to land reform, that they had a golden opportunity to accomplish long-term ideals in one master stroke. Thus motivated, they overlooked the realities of social and political behavior in the country and exaggerated the capability even of dictatorial power to produce change. Their actions—a good example of idealistic outside-in planning—created drains and confusions that hampered progress in a noble cause.

Nature of Key Talents and Abilities

The heart of the inside-out approach is the appraisal of unique talents, abilities, aptitudes, and resources possessed by the organization (or by that particular part of the organization involved in carrying out the plan). If this appraisal is not done well, the choice of a goal cannot be made well. There is often a temptation for leaders to see only those key abilities that they wish to see or to imagine talents that they wish their organizations had.

To counteract this temptation, it is desirable to use quantitative measures wherever appropriate. What do the figures for current and past performance indicate about organizational talents? In an impressive number of business companies in the United States and other Western nations, executives are making increased use of techniques for eliminating irrelevant figures or variables and picking out the data that really tell the story. For instance, some companies have found ways to "zero in" on the return obtained from dollars spent on advertising; this has meant cutting through a good deal of "static" and "random interference" resulting from events that happen to stimulate or depress the results of an advertising campaign (seasonal slumps in shopping, for instance, or fluctuations in response because of general economic conditions, or the fact that a competitor launched a major new promotion at the same time). Other companies have worked out ingenious indices of the productivity of their scientific and engineering people and then compared their own productivity data with that for other companies. The temptation to wishful thinking can also be counteracted by obtaining the judgments of good outside consultants. Organizations like Arthur D. Little, Inc., McKinsey & Company, and Booz, Allen & Hamilton, for example, have for years given corporate management teams objective, professional appraisals of strengths and weaknesses.

Nevertheless, there is no getting around the fact that an organizational self-appraisal can rarely be made without making judgments based in part on what executives call "gut feel." This is as it should be. Highly personal, subjective values and attitudes may be an important aspect, we shall see, of the organization's profile of unique talents and resources. First, though, let us look at the more obvious talents that should be scrutinized in an appraisal.

TANGIBLE ABILITIES

One important kind of strength to look for is know-how. What does the organization know how to do better than most other organizations it will have to contend with? More than most types of ability, unique skills may enable planners to find great opportunities in surprisingly new areas for the company or agency. A dramatic case in point is the aerospace companies—North American Aviation, TRW, Lockheed, Aerojet-General, and others. In their contract work for NASA and the Department of Defense, these companies developed extraordinary skills in systems engineering. After applying these skills for a number of years solely to space vehicles, launching and guidance systems, and military hardware, they realized they possessed an ability of great value in other fields in which it is important to deal with many complex and interrelated factors. Hence we have seen Aerojet-General undertaking the study of waste management for Fresno County in California, Lockheed working out new operating systems for hospitals and medical centers, Tempo (General Electric Company's group in Santa Barbara) working out plans to restructure an old city and establish a new one, Space-General Corporation doing contract work on crime prevention and social welfare systems, and other aerospace companies engaged in still other projects.

Another vital kind of ability concerns the orientation of people in the company or agency. Are they "efficiency minded"? Do they like repetition? Do they like to be first in a new field instead of second? Do they revel in detail work? Are they willing to pay the price of keeping in personal touch with the customer? Crown Cork & Seal Company is a wonderful example of this last ability. Although overshadowed in size by its giant rivals, American Can Company and Continental Can Company, it has long been a highly profitable company. The secret of its success seems to be a top executive team that is glad to deal on a phone call's notice day or night with the smallest details of customer service, that is willing to work long hours and forego vacations in order to provide such service, that can make decisions fast and move swiftly to sell a new prospect, and that has a genius for keeping costs to a minimum.[5] Such a set of talents has highly significant implications for any planning effort undertaken. It affects the kinds of recruitment and personnel programs which are desirable, the kinds of customers and businesses which the company should seek in the future, and also, of course, the kind of corporate planning itself which is desirable in the company (for instance, the time span covered, the amount of detail, the forms of evaluation sought, and the question of staff assistance in planning).

Still another type of tangible ability is knowledge or possession of strategically vital resources. In 1966 and 1967, when nearly every major railroad in the country was working overtime to get out of the passenger business, the Pennsylvania Railroad Company under Stuart T. Sanders was rebuilding its 226-mile line between Washington and New York City, retraining four thousand employees for this service, and making heavy investments in new self-propelled Budd cars. As of this writing, the outcome of the program is not known, but whether or not it is successful, it represents in intelligent attempt at inside-out planning. In undertaking this program, Sanders and his planners seek to exploit an unusual resource of the Pennsylvania Railroad—the fact that it alone possesses the ground-level rights of way between Washington and New York, that the organization's knowledge of the railroad business is unique, and that these two resources in combination could produce a form of high-speed transit that a large segment of the growing New York–Washington commuter population would prefer to airline travel or highway transportation.

INTANGIBLE FACTORS

No less important than apparent skills and abilities are the less visible, subtle characteristics of people in the organization—their

[5] See *Forbes,* April 15, 1964, pp. 47–48.

values, aptitudes, and "state of mind." It is not easy to take these into account. But taken into account they must be, if planners hope to choose strategic goals wisely. Fortunately, behavioral scientists are pointing to useful ways of assessing such intangibles and helping planners to recognize them by presenting concrete case examples from past experience. In some companies these ways are being used profitably, and in other firms there are managers who possess and use great native abilities to assess people's values. Generally speaking, however, it appears that planning leaders have not paid nearly enough attention to intangible factors in the past. I know of no formal planning documents in which such considerations are spelled out (although they may have been in the minds of the decision makers).

Would personal values have a substantial impact on the choice of goals if they were considered? Consider an actual case. Several years ago, William D. Guth and Renato Tagiuri report,[6] the top management of a large research and development corporation was pondering possible strategies for the future. One possibility was very rapid growth based on ventures into space research; a second was moderate growth based on developing current products (a high proportion of them produced for the government); and a third was rapid growth based on developing commercial applications of company research. The president and his three top officers discussed these different goals a number of times but could reach no agreement on them; each of the three subordinates espoused a different strategy. The president himself favored the first alternative but hesitated to designate it for fear it would not be supported enthusiastically. In order to make up his mind, he examined the different personal values held by his top officers. He saw one of them as placing great importance on a stimulating research atmosphere for the company; another valued practical scientific progress most; the third primarily interested in rapid commercial expansion and increased profitability. With these contrasts in mind, the president decided on the second strategy of moderate growth based on developing the present

[6] *Op. cit.*, pp. 123–124.

product lines. He felt that this strategy best matched the values of his top executives *as a team*. His decision turned out to be a wise one; the strategy proved to be successful, and the president remained well satisfied with his choice.

As Guth and Tagiuri point out, people are prone to exaggerate the values of others. Their study of one thousand men shows, for example, that scientists and research managers believe general executives to be considerably more concerned with "economic" criteria and considerably less influenced by "religious" standards than the executives believe themselves to be. People are also prone, Guth and Tagiuri point out, to adopt just the opposite attitude on occasion, taking it for granted that others hold the same values as they do. Making accurate assessments of values, therefore, cannot be done hastily. One must look critically at himself: what values are important to him? Then he can better allow for his own biases in evaluating the ideals of other people. In deducing the value assumptions of others from their recommendations and beliefs concerning desirable goals, he should make appropriate allowances, if he can, for different interpretations by them of the facts at hand (did they use different estimates of the probable cost of a new process, let us say, or of its usefulness in a certain market?). In addition he can also learn something of his own and others' values from certain kinds of tests.[7]

Another useful procedure is preference theory (also called utility theory). This is a means of determining a person's attitudes toward risk—to what extent he is a gambler willing to "go for broke," or a conservative who tends to wait for a "sure thing," or one who "plays the odds." Such attitudes are determined by asking the person a carefully designed sequence of questions concerning his willingness to take a chance under certain circumstances; methods of validating the resulting preference curve have also been worked out. Preference theory is useful not only for assessing one's attitudes toward risk but also for communicating desired risk attitudes to others in an organization.

[7] *Ibid.*, p. 129.

"Inner-Directedness" in Planning

The beauty of inside-out planning is that it is tailored to what people can do, do do, and have confidence in doing. It emphasizes the possibilities of playing from an organization's demonstrated personal strength rather than taking chances on estimates of the market, industry, or environment.

The inside-out method requires continuing appraisals of organizational talents and resources, just as the outside-in approach calls for continuing analyses of market conditions, economic trends, and/or other environmental factors. However, organizational talents do not change as rapidly as one might think—and certainly not nearly so rapidly as external conditions do. For while the particular products and processes an organization makes may go out of date fast, its profile of abilities and attitudes—its "personality," so to speak—tends to persist for years on end.

Inside-out rests on the assumption that to a large extent a business can create a market by what it does, if it does the job well, or that an educational or public organization can create opportunities for service, if it approaches the task well. It is for this reason that the inside-out approach may lead to different objectives from outside-in, because in the latter approach the forecaster looks only at trends already generated, not at new trends that *might* be generated by a creative company or agency. To the inside-outer, the first and most creative step in goal-setting is, as one executive once told me, "finding out how to do the most with what we are good at." A manager of sales and distribution planning for a well-known American company put it in another way. The need, he said, was to put more stress on the question, "What do we do to make what we want to happen, happen?" and less stress on asking the forecaster, "What should happen?"[8]

[8] Ernest C. Miller, *Marketing Planning,* AMA Research Study 81 (New York, American Management Association, 1967), p. 89.

CHAPTER 8

Building in the Right Action

THE SELECTION of broad goals and strategies is one part of planning; the choice of steps and means for achieving these goals is another. We come here to what is perhaps the most interesting question of all. How can a plan of action for attaining a goal be designed so as to enlist employees' support and enthusiasm?

Almost all planners and students of planning will readily agree that a program of action should contain incentives or "motivators" for the people who will carry out the work. Typically, however, these provisions are added to the package *after* considerable effort has gone into figuring out the necessary measures for financing, purchasing, building, installing equipment, organizing work staffs, handling the legal aspects, and similar matters necessary to attain the desired goal. In other words, the human incentives come in as a kind of afterthought—or, as I have sometimes heard men say, as "sweeteners" designed to make the plan more palatable to its implementers. The notion seems to be that making a new program workable is somewhat like making a controversial bill passable in a legislature; if, at the end of the bill, you can just tack on enough concessions or special riders to placate the opposition, you can bull your way through.

This is one of the great fallacies of planning. In reality, the human side is not "brought in" by planners; it is there *all the time*. The question is not *whether* management's program should include additional provisions designed to motivate people, but *how* provisions already included affect people. Not a few, not some, but a great many of the steps and procedures normally included in a program have implications for human action—even though no thought at all may be given to those implications when the program is drawn up.

To use an analogy, a program of action for accomplishing an objective is like a coin. It has two sides—the physical resources side and the "people" side. If either side is left blank in the designing, the program is as imperfect as a coin printed only on one side. Just as such a coin is not negotiable, so the plan is likely to be taken "out of circulation" after a while.

What kinds of steps and provisions commonly used to implement plans have vital implications for employee behavior? This is the question we shall look at in this chapter.

Inevitable Human Consequences

STARTING TIME

Even before any financial, organizational, or marketing method begins to affect the success of a plan of action, the die has begun to be cast as a result of another factor. That is the starting time. Generally speaking, it appears that plans, like news, must be timely if they are to capture people's attention and enlist a response. There must be a recognized need to do something. If the organization is a company that is falling behind competitors in technology, profitability, or market position, people in the company must feel concerned about this trend or be afraid of its consequences for them. If the organization is a college whose faculty is torn by dissension and dissatisfaction, there must be a strong feeling on the part of deans and influential teachers that something must be done about the problem.

In a study of a series of business cases in which organizational change succeeded and failed, Larry E. Greiner found that the presence or absence of felt pressures and dissatisfactions had a

decisive impact on business executives' efforts to reorganize or revise operations.[1] The chances for success were best, he concluded,
if the pressures reflected both events outside the organization
(e.g., stockholder discontent) and events inside it (e.g., high
costs). In an illustrative case of success he cited, the managers of
a plan were being bombarded by urgent telephone calls, tele-
grams, letters, and memoranda from corporate headquarters, and
were also sensitive about the poor performance record of the
plant as compared to other plants and divisions.

Actually the question is not whether a plan for change is timely
as measured by objective criteria, but whether it *seems* timely
to the people involved. Organization leaders have considerable
influence over this question. They have almost unquestioned
power to communicate various information and to dramatize
certain needs and events. Astute labor leaders know this and are
past masters at the art of making union members acutely con-
scious of certain needs so that when a program of action is
launched, the time *will* be right for it as far as workers are concerned.

STARTING PLACE

In many instances, programs do not start as massive, all-out
assaults. They begin selectively, in a modest way, building up
momentum as they go along. The decision about *where* to undertake these initial operations has human consequences, just as
does the decision about the time of launching.

Bruce Payne, a veteran authority on cost-reduction programs,
once pointed out how important it is to choose the right jobs and
groups for the start of a new program; often there will be such
opposition to change that the best-thought-out plan will have
little chance if launched in many areas of the plant. Payne urged
starting with a very ordinary operation employing but a few
people, one that was somewhat out of the way, could be learned
quickly, and had a good supervisor. Assuming the plan produced

[1] *Op. cit.*, pp. 124–125.

desirable results, operators around the area could then begin *seeing* its advantages and *selling themselves* on its desirability.

There is a kind of universality about this principle, at least, in the case of those plans which can be introduced selectively and where hostility to change is a major factor. In the Third Plan for Iran, mentioned earlier, which was intended to support economic growth during the period 1962–1967, the planners calculated a whole series of gains that could be achieved by introducing improved seeds, fertilizers, pesticides, soil-working methods, cow breeding, and other practices. The two keys to getting these ideas used, they decided, were communicating the necessary know-how to the landlords and cultivators who made production decisions and providing ready access to credit so that the needed supplies could be purchased. At the same time, however, they appreciated that the government had limited resources for implementing the plan—and, equally important, that not all Iranians saw the value of new agricultural methods. So they elected to begin in areas where there seemed to be the most cultivators who possessed incentives to improve farm production, and where conditions in general were most favorable.[2] In other words, the planners wanted to be sure that the potential pay-offs of the program would become visible clearly and quickly. They wanted the "word-of-mouth" factor to begin operating in the plan's favor as soon as possible. In such an approach lay the best hope of ultimately getting all farmers to use the most effective techniques of production.

DECISION-MAKING POWERS

One of the most interesting aspects of planning is where and how to place responsibility for the decision-making necessary to carry out the program. One thing is certain: however planning leaders decide (or fail to decide) such questions, the result will affect human action in some way. The only matter for con-

[2] See Baldwin, *op. cit.,* pp. 76, 84–85, 89–92.

jecture is whether cooperation and enthusiasm will be influenced favorably or unfavorably.

Often management elects to give certain key men large, un-fettered powers of decision-making in carrying out the program. Various heads of divisions and departments down the line may be made virtual czars or dictators, endowed with great authority to manage operations in the manner they see fit. In some situations this may be a very wise move. In one such situation the ad-vantages of swift, bold action outweigh the risk of local tyranny and high costs of operation. In another such situation the goals of the plan are of a black-or-white nature, so that an operating head's progress toward the goal can be readily evaluated. In World War II, General Douglas MacArthur received enormous powers in the Pacific campaign. General George Marshall, Secre-tary Henry Stimson, President Roosevelt, and others in Wash-ington were continually on the receiving end of bitter complaints from other military leaders in the Pacific, from the Allies, and from civilians about the arbitrary decisions and policies Mac-Arthur made. But Marshall, Stimson, and Roosevelt were of one mind—most of the time, at any rate—that it was better to have a leader who could win the Pacific war as rapidly as possible than one who, while proceeding more rationally and tactfully, would produce victories at a slower rate. Much the same might be said of Lincoln's decisions to stick with Grant during the last half of the Civil War. Similarly, in industry, top management may gladly opt for a division head who will get the operation out of the red quickly, even though he is ruthless with the people in-volved, rather than a man who will improve operations less rapidly but with greater justice and fairness to all involved.

But swift, decisive action is not always so important. Top management's strategy may be more subtle—and in that case the "czar approach" may not be suitable at all. Several years ago I had a talk with a couple of executives at Philips, the great Dutch-based electronics corporation (N. V. Philips Gloeilampenfa-brieken of Eindhoven). They told me that the strategy of this company was usually to let others be first in opening a new market and then, when the market showed signs of fast growth, come in with its new products. Philips had a liberal research budget and had built up a fine reputation for its research and development strength. But it chose to blend its R&D potentials with a strong instinct for commercialization which often told it to "wait and see." What kind of decision-making pattern did Philips have to implement this strategy? Each division had twin heads—a "technical" man and a "commercial" man, each accountable for the entire operation of the division. This unique pattern was believed quite important in the company's success. The twin heads acted as checks on each other; the technical man assured that the division was in the forefront in research and engineering and did not become too cautious, while the commercial man saw to it that the division did not go overboard with ambitious new products or jeopardize profitability by trying to pioneer in new technologies.[3]

In 1967 in South Vietnam, General William C. Westmoreland was assigned the task of directing the so-called Pacification Program to build up the economic, political, and social strength of the villages. Civilians in Vietnam became alarmed that the military organization would dominate and rule out socio-economic viewpoints. To answer this objection, Robert Komer, Westmoreland's deputy for the Pacification Program, arranged that if the number-one man in any area were a military person, the number-two man should be a civilian, and vice versa. Here again a system of organizational checks and balances was seen necessary to implement a strategy that blended somewhat contradictory principles and ideals.

SUPERVISORY STYLES

In recent years readers of management literature have become acquainted with many possible managerial styles—"benevolent autocracy," "theories X and Y," "participative management," and

[3] For a fuller account of Philips' approach, see *International Management*, March, 1965, pp. 17–20.

others. To a certain extent this matter is related to the question of the proper amount of authority, just discussed, but it is different in emphasis: it has more to do with superior-subordinate relationships in the *execution* of authority, whether the authority is small or great.

It is amazing that planners in general have not paid more attention to the vital connection between supervisory style and the implementation of strategic programs (as if the one, having to do with management, were separable from the other, having to do with planning). Certainly the secret was out years ago. In the early growth period of Eastman Kodak, for example, the company had a high goal for quality control. Management recognized that its long-range hopes for volume depended in part on the confidence prospective buyers had in the film sold. But in those days reliability of photographic film could not be ensured, as it is today, by automatic equipment in the darkroom. The company had to count on employees to *volunteer* information about defects in the film produced or processes used. What could be done to make employees willing to do that? Realizing that the general environment and climate of the work place was a key factor, the company developed a system of permissive and participative management that later became famous.

In a more contemporary case, the management of a supermarket chain worked out a program of decentralizing authority to pave the way for long-range increases in volume and profits. One of the things decentralization meant was more influence and power for store managers. Previously they had been glorified errand boys for the district managers (the latter were men who oversaw operations for several stores in an area). Now they were asked to do more of the decision-making themselves. To accomplish this change in behavior, top management decided on two changes in procedure for budgeting and employee rating: (1) when the district manager was making up the budget, he was to ask (not tell) his store manager what his sales and expense forecasts were; (2) when the district manager was making out the reports on employees, he was to ask (not tell) his store manager how he rated the men and women under him.

As Paul Lawrence, the author of this study, points out, this procedural change was no guarantee that behavior would change in the desired way; the district manager could still go on dominating the store manager's thinking or disregarding it when it did not agree with his own. Nevertheless, the new policy tended to push managers in the direction desired. Over time it could be expected to lead district managers to place more trust in the thinking of the store heads and lead the store heads to develop different notions of their own jobs and functions. In addition, top management set up a new system of meetings between managers at different levels, with store managers being asked to speak out more than they had in the past.[4]

In a large company, university, government agency, or other organization, this matter of supervisory style may take on especial interest because of the variety needed *within* the organization. One leading manufacturer has a food division and a chemical products division. The company, being planning minded, insists on long-range programs for each division. In the food division, the time required to go from research on a new food product to full distribution ranges from two-and-one-half to four-and-one-half years; advertising is a large and decisive part of the cost dollar; marketing men rule operations; promotion for a good manager is rapid. In such a division, the "top-down" style of management may work well in the implementation of programs. In the chemical products division, by contrast, quite a different situation prevails. The lead time from research on a new product to commercialization may range up to seven years; the research budget is about twice as large as for other company divisions; and technical people are crucial not only in research and laboratory service operations but also in sales, in which they and salesmen work closely with users. In such a division, a "bottom-up" style is likely to be necessary if ambitious product development programs are to succeed. A good research supervisor will be given considerable discretion and leeway in operations, and, while expected to work within a framework of planned objectives, he will be given con-

[4] See *The Changing of Organizational Behavior Patterns* (Boston, Harvard Business School Division of Research, 1958), especially pp. 67 and 187–188.

siderable independence to pursue his technical interests. (If he does not receive such independence, he will probably leave for some other company.)

To sum up, the question of supervisory style is particularly significant in planning because every work group, every production or marketing operation, every division must have *some* pattern of boss-worker relationships. Is the pattern developed suitable for carrying out the goals that are set? And are the programs selected consistent with the supervisory styles employed? Inevitably the styles will affect the plan. The plan *can*, in turn, affect the styles. The sophisticated planner will try to work it both ways.

LOCATION OF OFFICES AND FACILITIES

Just as planning is affected by the manner in which managers and employees work together, so is it affected by the matter of *where* they work. Are the different departments involved in the program located close together or far apart? Will the people see each other frequently as they go about their work or not at all? Whatever the answer, the prospects for swift, effective implementation of the program are increased or decreased as a result.

If a high degree of coordination is desirable for several groups, then physical proximity is desirable. The more contacts the groups have—informal contacts in the lunchroom, in the corridors, during commuting, and so forth, as well as formal contacts during meetings—the greater the probability that one will know what the other is doing and why. From this knowledge there tends to develop over a period of time a certain sharing of assumptions about the future, of values important to progress, and of goals worth striving for. Such coordination and shared thinking may be extremely important to the success of a program. A company's new product hopes may rest on whether the marketing and production groups can move in unison with a minimum of waste motion—and all the work of official coordinators, "integrators," and joint committees will be of little avail unless there is also a kind of family or team spirit between marketing and production, which can only be created with easy physical contact. Eaxmples of such a need are numerous in industry, education, government, and other fields.

But planning leaders do not always want such a rich blend of thinking and action. Formal, top-down coordination may suffice. In fact, management may look in a negative way at close collaboration, referring to it in a disparaging way as "groupthink." It may seem more important that two groups or divisions proceed with a high degree of independence and individualism. Harold Ross, the great editor of *The New Yorker,* was a fervent believer in the complete divorce of the editorial and business departments of his magazine; the less the two intertwined in planning and operations, the better, from his standpoint. And in many corporations today there is a firm belief that there should be a good distance between the people in basic research and the people working on "applied research" or "development," because the kinds of attitudes and philosophies required are so different. In fact, one company made a special effort to locate its laboratories for fundamental research on the West Coast so that those researchers would rarely be influenced by the development engineers, production people, and marketing experts in the Midwest offices.

Not always, of course, is close collaboration seen as all bad or all good. Sometimes a little of both collaboration and independence may be sought, and some ingenious schemes have been devised to this end. Bell Telephone Laboratories wanted to keep its basic and applied research groups separate on the organization chart; each was made to report and be accountable to different offices in the hierarchy. At the same time, Bell Labs wanted each group to take advantage of any knowledge possessed by the other that would help it accomplish its own unique objectives. The organizational barriers to such pooling of knowledge were overcome by housing basic and applied research in the same building, so that researchers in the two groups would find it natural to develop informal contacts and transfer knowledge back and forth. Scientists in each laboratory had the same status in the company, which helped this process of communication.[5]

SIZE OF GROUPS AND DEPARTMENTS

Another factor that has a bearing on the execution of a program is the size of the groups, departments, and divisions involved in the work. Size in turn is generally a reflection of the volume or complexity of operations. When the aim of a plan is to double or triple the volume of business or engage the organization in new lines of endeavor in which a multitude of diverse skills, talents, and resources must be brought to bear, then vital tactical questions should be raised about group size. Do key managers have the ability to direct the larger volume of operations contemplated? If they do not, can that ability be developed in them by training programs? If not, should executives with the needed abilities be brought in from outside (which in turn raises human relations questions)? Or perhaps best of all, is there a practical way of so splitting up the work, of dividing the assignments, that the impact on group size is not great?

Between 1952 and 1961, the Ryder System, Inc., expanded prodigiously in sales volume from $3 million to $105.3 million. It accomplished this feat by expanding its trucking business and adding truck-leasing operations; most of its competitors were in one or the other, but not both. It had become, by 1961, the country's second-largest truck-leasing firm and the seventh-largest trucker. It became apparent, however, that the large staffs of people necessary to handle this business could not be directed effectively by top executives. Instead of becoming more profitable, Ryder System began incurring losses—$228,000 in 1961. "We found," James A. Ryder told a *Forbes* reporter, "that our people could handle the business when it was $10 million in gross volume but when it got close to $60 million, they couldn't. It sounds like the same principles would apply but they didn't."[6] So in 1964

[5] See Sumner Myers, "Technology Transfer and Industrial Innovation," *Looking Ahead* (National Planning Association), February, 1967, p. 3.
[6] *Forbes*, December 15, 1965, p. 37.

management sold off the carrier part of the business. Concentrating on truck leasing only, it was making a fine profit showing again within a year.

Anticipating problems of this kind, the planner can consider various possible solutions. If the organization shows signs of strain, it may be practical to set off one or more of the expanded operations as a subsidiary company. The executives to handle the subsidiary might be brought in from outside the company, given considerable independence, and made accountable only for profit results. Another possibility would be to plan to expand in the new line of business through a joint venture; that is, instead of going it alone, the company might team up with another company that is also interested in the new business, pool resources with it, and thus share the burden instead of shouldering it alone. Thus, Time Incorporated and General Electric Company got together to create General Learning Corporation, a new venture in the educational field. Time contributed Silver Burdett Company, a textbook manufacturer that had been wholly owned by Time, and GE contributed $18,750,000 in working capital. Conceivably, General Learning could have been created and managed by either Time or GE alone. But the resulting strain on both the human and material sides of either company might have been dangerously high.

INFORMATION AND COMMUNICATION

After a new program goes into operation, it is frequently important to gather and disseminate certain information—figures with which to evaluate progress, facts indicating the time for beginning another stage of operations, data for use in revising the plan, and so forth. This information function has become so important, with all the emphasis now placed on knowledge in management, that executives in charge of planning may provide expressly for it in the program itself or tacitly assume that it will be handled in such-and-such a way. Such provisions and assumptions are likely to have no small bearing on the outcome. Perhaps the three most important questions for planners to consider are:

1. Who will gather needed information?
2. To whom and how readily will it be made available?
3. To which individuals and groups will reports be sent regularly through formal channels?

These and other questions are dealt with in detail by the burgeoning literature on management-information systems. The following are a few interesting issues from the standpoint of plan implementation.

Who will obtain the data? Much information needed for carrying out plans is, of course, collected as a matter of routine. An example is data showing whether or not production volume is changing as planned. But often the information needed calls for a special fact-finding mission. A joint venture that was expected to do well seems to be failing. Why? And what revisions in the program should be made as a result? An unexpected change in the marketing picture develops. How significant is it for the company? Does it mean that the goals of the plan should be revised?

There is nothing new about questions of this nature and their impact on planning. One may understandably be amazed, however, at how commonly it is assumed that the only problem is to get the "right" answer. Getting the "right" answer is only part of the problem. *How* the data are gathered and *by whom* are crucial matters. In many cases management would be further ahead if a 75 percent correct answer were obtained in a suitable way by the right people than if a 100 percent correct answer were obtained in the wrong way by the wrong people. In the former case, there is a good chance the data will be acted on, promptly and with enthusiasm; in the latter case, there is not.

Let me illustrate with a simple example. A company sees expanding markets for one of its products and decides to invest in the new plant and equipment necessary for greater production. The desired goal for increased output can be met in two years if there is no shortage of qualified workers, but a shortage may indeed occur, in which case the desired goal may not be attainable for three or four years. "*But,*" the marketing people argue, "we could fill the new jobs if we loosened our requirements for job applicants and did more on-the-job training." The production people—especially the quality control men—do not want to do that; they would much prefer to have the increases in output postponed. "You don't realize," they insist, "what chaos is created when mistakes are made with the equipment." After hearing the two sides argued, the planning heads decide that *if* a labor shortage develops, an outside consultant will be called in to recommend for or against relaxing the standards for job applicants.

This may be the way to get the "right" answer in a technical sense (assuming the outside expert knows his stuff), but consider the implications for the human side of planning. Judging from past experience, there is a high probability that production will ignore the outsider's recommendation, if it is for loosening standards—or perhaps even sabotage it.

Now suppose the planners leave it up to a committee of production people to investigate the effects of loosening applicant standards and trying to compensate with more in-plant training? It will be argued by marketing men that production is so biased it will find out what it "wants" to find. Certainly there is a risk of this happening. But is it a prohibitive risk? On countless occasions in the past the factual justification for a policy change has come from a department's own fact-finding group. (It is not change that people resist, but *being* changed.) This could happen in our case example, assuming there are really good arguments for the proposed departure. If it does happen, management can be confident that production people will follow through on the recommendation and carry it out swiftly.

How readily accessible will data be? This question can arise in all types of situations. Even in a small organization, a special effort may have to be made to assure that one office can quickly get needed information that is available elsewhere in the building. But the question is mostly likely to rate the attention of planners in an organization in which operations are scattered about at different points. More than one military campaign has been lost because no ways were set up ahead of time to enable officers in one sector to ascertain readily what had happened in another sector; more than one corporate plan has suffered because managers working on one segment could not learn quickly enough what had been accomplished on another segment; and plans of churches and colleges have been dealt "crushers" for similar reasons.

IBM did not fall victim to this error in the early stages of engineering the System/360. The design of this pioneering new computer concept, in developing which the company gambled much of its reputation, leadership position, and financial treasure, was to be worked out in a number of different laboratories in the early 1960's. IBM's lab at Hursley, England, was assigned the job of developing the model 30; four of the original model designs were to be done at Poughkeepsie, New York; at one stage, assignments went to labs in Germany; and other locations also were involved. Because the giant undertaking had to be done under great time pressures, management saw that it would be highly important to provide any one lab with virtually instant access to information and developments in the others. Management planners therefore arranged to lease a special trans-Atlantic line between United States labs and the labs abroad. "The international engineering group was woven together with considerable effectiveness," reports *Fortune*, "giving IBM the justifiable claim that the 360 computer was probably the first product of truly international design."[7]

Who will receive regular reports? Because ambitious plans almost invariably mean that new kinds of decisions must be made at various action centers, they also mean that managers must receive different kinds of information to act upon. Special attention to regular reporting procedures therefore seems like an obvious requirement in any major program. In practice, however, the requirement seems often not to be met. Why?

For one thing, there is likely to be an objection to changing or enlarging the reporting system. When the medium-sized super-

---

[7] T. A. Wise, "The Rocky Road to the Marketplace," *Fortune*, October, 1966, p. 142.

market chain referred to earlier planned to give more authority and power to the managers of the different stores, as part of a program to decentralize decision-making, one of the vice-presidents thought it would be helpful to feed the store managers current information on any union contract negotiations in progress. Objections to this move came from one executive with whom the vice-president talked. Such information had previously been kept confidential for top management because of the danger of "leaks," the vice-president was reminded. If just one store manager started talking to a union representative about the information from headquarters, the company would be in hot water. The vice-president overrode the objection and went ahead with the idea, not because he saw no possibility of risk but because he felt the risk was worth taking if store managers were to practice the new roles given them in the decentralization plan. This is an illustration of the kind of trade-off which time and time again the planner must be willing to make if the informational requirements of a new program are to be met.

Secondly, a changed reporting system calls for "elbow grease," and if executives who must do the work are for any reason not dedicated to the plan (as when it is foisted on them by overbearing senior or overzealous staff specialists), it is all too tempting to avoid the necessary effort. In the early 1920's, Alfred P. Sloan, Jr., was one of those at General Motors who felt concerned about the lack of contact between the company's corporate research division (then at Dayton, Ohio) and the engineering and research groups of the car divisions. This communication gap had aggravated a very bitter fight over the merits of the copper-cooled engine; more importantly, it handicapped corporate efforts to reach long-range goals for improved engineering and sales. Sloan's solution in 1923 was the creation of a general technical committee. The committee regularly brought together the car divisions' chief engineers and Charles Kettering's corporate staff engineers. The committee meetings produced many good results, including the dissemination of information on technical developments and progress; these gains in turn helped

GM to reach its goals. Sloan's idea was simple, uncomplicated, and supported by the power of his office; yet it by no means had automatic acceptance in management. Sloan nurtured the idea in his own mind for some time, discussed it with associates, presented it to a meeting of car division managers and group vice-presidents, wrote a 1,500-word memorandum on it which he circulated to a number of other corporate executives, arranged for the committee's expenses to be met out of the corporate budget, and sat in on many of the first meetings of the committee. The meetings sometimes extended into a weekend of golf and fishing, which pleased Sloan because he felt informality helped the men exchange views with one another.[8]

Time, Inc., which is also a planning-minded company, uses the informality of executive lunches to help speed the flowing back and forth of ideas pertinent to planning. During a typical week an executive will attend several lunches hosted by other executives at Time, and every other week or so he will himself host a lunch for a certain managerial group. These lunch meetings are not used by seniors to clarify instructions for subordinates or to give lectures, but to give the people attending a better chance to learn from one another. This process is considered particularly important at Time because the main responsibility for planning is on operating executives; there is no formal planning department made up of staff specialists.[9]

DEADLINES

Even the deadline set for completion of a program can affect the human side of the ledger. The time may be an ambitious one, an easy target, or perhaps left indefinite. In any of these cases, depending on the circumstances, it may advance or retard the aims of the plan. Most research managers, I suspect, would deem it best to leave deadlines ambiguous in the case of a basic scientific

[8] See Sloan's book, *My Years With General Motors* (Garden City, Doubleday & Company, Inc., 1964), pp. 105–108.

[9] See Time Incorporated, Intercollegiate Clearing House Case 12C14—BC 290 (Harvard Business School).

inquiry in which the outlines of the problem are vague, the kinds of probing necessary are only poorly understood, and just a general notion of the ultimate value of the project can be entertained. By contrast, in most kinds of development work or "applied" research—and in hundreds of other ventures, from planning the introduction of a new product to reorganizing a management information system—it would clearly be a mistake not to set very clear target dates.

An ambitious or very early target date *may* tempt people down the line to make shortcuts, as in the case of the division manager who is under such pressure to produce results early that he "cheats" on activities that would be beneficial in the long run (management training, say, or staff work) and concentrates only on making a good short-run showing. In other circumstances, however, an early deadline may have just the opposite effect. After the ill-fated Apollo capsule fire on January 27, 1967, which killed astronauts Grissom, White, and Chaffee, NASA officials were queried about their 1969 deadline for a moon landing. Had the ambitiousness of it caused too much haste in executing the moon program? The NASA heads thought not; in fact, they argued, the early deadline had tended to inspire great effort and helped NASA to attract the most talented experts to work on the program.

Obviously everything depends on the nature of the mission as people perceive it—and to a considerable extent that is a function of management's ability to dramatize the objective and influence people's perceptions of it. During the early stages of World War II, General MacArthur became noted for giving his subordinates deadlines for completing an action that seemed virtually impossible to meet. But MacArthur had an unusual ability to dramatize a mission (and, some observers felt, actually to frighten subordinate commanders who objected to a target date); also, of course, he had the overriding importance of the Allied cause working in his favor. On the other hand, there are innumerable organizations in this country which not only lack MacArthurs in their leadership but do not undertake missions that can be readily dramatized; for them to try to do what the five-star general did would be folly.

Summary

Nearly all the steps of implementing a program are fraught with consequences for human endeavor. This is true whether the planning leaders decide about these steps in a formal written document, in various memoranda, in conversations—or not at all. In one way or another, assumptions must be made. The human side may be handled well or poorly. Practically never, however, is it unaffected by the action taken.

THE RACE is not always to the swift, nor the battle to the strong—but that's the way to bet.

—DAMON RUNYAN

CHAPTER 9

Total Mobilization

IF THE PLANNING MOVEMENT had a hall of fame, it would have to include Alfred the Great. During his reign as king of England, invasion from Denmark was a continuous threat. The Danes struck at Wessex four times between 871 and 878. They were brave, efficient, and cruel fighters (as were the English), and at one time they occupied an area to the north of London which was nearly as large as the domain under Alfred's influence. The Danish invasions struck terror in the hearts of many of Alfred's people; the fact that, having no intelligence system, the Britons never knew from week to week when the next invasion fleet would come in sight, added to the psychological damage.

Realizing that the security of his kingdom called for more than courage and weaponry on the battlefield, Alfred undertook a long-range defense program that, considering conditions in his day, surpassed in ambition, scope, and imagination anything done since then in western Europe. He directed the construction of a great system of fortified strongholds around Wessex. This system —so ambitious it could not be finished during his reign—was one of the keys to his last great and successful defense against the Danes during the years 892–896. The forts or "burhs," as they were called, which comprised the system were to enable native Britons in the immediate area of an invasion to hold up a surprise attack until reinforcements could come to their rescue. Secondly, Alfred built and trained a national army. The well-disciplined, mobile forces that made up this army were assigned to sectors; the army's task was to move swiftly, confront an invasion group, and repel it before it could establish itself.

Lesser planners than Alfred might have stopped at this point. Alfred went further and in so doing demonstrated a principle of enduring value to planners. One major problem he foresaw was to keep the walls of the burhs in good repair—no mean problem in view of the horrendous difficulties of control and supervision during that period. Alfred's solution was to assign specific people to the task, give them a specific time to do it, and motivate them in terms of narrow self-interest as well as of patriotic duty. The task of keeping a burh in good repair was to be done by the farmers in the immediate area; they were to make any necessary repairs during the fortnight after the so-called Regation Days, a time that usually fell in May when there was a comparatively slack period for farmers. In return for doing these duties, "the men who kept the burh," as described in the official documents, were exempt from service away from home in the national army.

To make this "positive" incentive more meaningful, as well as to make the national army itself more efficient, Alfred introduced a "negative" incentive: he tightened the requirements of military service. In the past a man had often been able to "escape the draft" by transferring allegiance from one lord to another; in this way he "kept ahead" of the recruiting officials. So Alfred had a law enacted (chapter 37 of his laws) requiring a man to inform his lord if he wished to transfer allegiance to another lord. This requirement was not foolproof, but it proved to be a reasonably effective solution.[1]

Alfred's success as a planner was due in no small part to his success in combining or integrating incentives in ways like the foregoing. To make sure that everything possible would be going for him, he blended both positive and negative "motiva-

[1] See P. J. Helm, *Alfred the Great* (New York, Thomas Y. Crowell Company, 1965), esp. pp. 104–109.

tors" to induce the kind of behavior needed to carry out the master plan.

Stated abstractly, the principle of integrated incentives and pressures seems so obvious that one would think no planner could fail to think of it. Yet untold programs have failed since Alfred's day because of failure to follow the principle— and countless programs seem doomed to fail today for the same reason. Several widely traveled management consultants say that it is a common occurrence, in their experience, for companies with plans for change to give salary increases to those who are change minded at the same rate as to those who are not, or to use methods that encourage the change (e.g., larger departmental budgets) as well as methods that do not (e.g., antiquated personnel policies). In government work such inconsistency seems to be inevitable because of tenure rules. In the Department of Defense, for instance, there were high-level officials under Secretary Robert McNamara who were intellectually and emotionally unequipped to implement the reorganization plans he undertook; perhaps he would have removed them if he could have, but the system prevented that.

If planning leaders are to get strong and enthusiastic support of programs for change, they must seek to shape all policies and practices so that the desired pattern of human behavior is continually encouraged and reinforced in every possible manner. Promotions, salary raises, bonus awards, recruitment practices, status symbols, assignments of responsibility and authority—all such practices must be directed so that people in the organization are influenced to act and think in the ways necessary for the goals to be achieved. The actions of one person or group on behalf of the program then become reinforced by the actions of other persons. With luck, there may even result a kind of synergistic effect—an overall organizational effort that is greater than the sum of the individual efforts.

In any event, the principle of coordinated, integrated practices means that planning leaders define exactly what kind of behavior is desired. Do they want managers and employees to allocate their time in different ways in order to support the plan properly? If so, precisely what priorities should be used? Do they want a certain viewpoint—engineering, say, or marketing—to prevail more often in the decisions and choices people make? If so, what kinds of considerations thereby become less important? These are the kinds of things that should be visualized on the human side of the planning ledger, just as buildings, facilities, and products are visualized on the physical resources side. To return to the example of King Alfred, in his long-range planning he must have had a mental picture of farmers dutifully repairing and maintaining the burhs in May and of members of the national army serving a little more gladly for the knowledge that relatively few of their countrymen were "escaping the draft." He must have visualized these and other behavioral patterns as well as ideas about weapons, numbers of fighting men, specifications of fortresses, and so on.

One may well ask at this point: if the steps and features of the program of action are well thought out in terms of their implications for human behavior (as discussed in the previous chapter), why is it necessary to do more? To answer can be stated briefly: (1) the steps in the plan can rarely be so well synchronized that they reinforce each other completely (for instance, the managers available for the new assignments may be "low-pressure" operators, whereas the deadlines for completion may call for "high-pressure" bosses); (2) in the early stages of a program, like the early stages of blast-off for a space shot, tremendous amounts of power may be needed to overcome inertia and develop momentum—and it may not be possible to generate such thrust within the confines of the plan of action itself; (3) therefore it is often necessary to support the program in other ways.

This reasoning may not apply to minor or specialized programs—the development of a new forecasting approach, let us say, or a new system of supervisory training—but it does generally hold for organization-wide, strategic programs. To use an analogy, when the United States fights a "local" war or "brush fire" overseas, the economy may go on operating as usual; most of the planning to be done concerns only the military services. But if the United States becomes involved in a major conflict like World War II, then total mobilization is required, and war planning encompasses the nation's economic machine, education, communications, and society at large. It is the "total mobilization" of a company's, agency's, or other organization's resources which will be examined in this chapter.

Developing a Coordinated Attack

Total mobilization begins, as the term suggests, with an examination of the whole gamut of activities which key managers and specialists are engaged in or should engage in. Are the policies and procedures being followed consistent with the objectives of the program? If not, how should they be changed so that they will be?

Let us look at an actual situation. In the container industry a company with annual sales of several hundred millions of dollars has attracted attention because of its unorthodox management. First, the company does not pay its top men high salaries and bonuses. Second, these men do not use the prime hours of the day for policy-making meetings; instead, just about all management meetings and conferences (and also travel) are conducted at night or on weekends. Third, by normal standards, the company's management group is understaffed: there are less than a dozen top people in the hierarchy. Fourth, executives have "open phones"; when they are working in their offices, they answer all telephone calls personally, with the secretaries being instructed to intercept calls only if their bosses are on other lines. Fifth, the company does not lavish money on research and advertising. Finally, it has stuck fairly consistently to its traditional product lines; there is relatively little interest in diversification.

Thus, this company breaks a whole set of textbook rules about "good management" and gets away with its unorthodoxy despite the fact it has large, powerful, and well-known competitors. In fact, its return on sales is greater than theirs, and it has been gaining in volume faster than they have been.

The secret of this company's success is an unusual capacity to serve customers quickly and efficiently and to move quickly when a new opportunity appears. The "open-phone" system means that a customer can call a top executive and get him right away any time he is in the office. The customer is treated with uncommon reverence when he calls, and managers are proud of giving him "small-company service" and using "small-company methods" despite their corporation being a large one. The way the management group operates means lightning-fast reaction times when a new piece of business is foreseen. "We move fast here, and we all make plenty of mistakes," one executive says. "But we at least move." Another executive says: "We're like an army with lots of sergeants with lots of rifles."

So much for what has been achieved. Now let us look at the method. Assuming that many an organization might like to create such a management pattern, how does it go about maintaining, strengthening, and intensifying the desired behavior? For one thing, if it wants its key people to act like entrepreneurs, it can help them (by options or other means) to acquire ownership interests. Significantly, in the company described, managers control nearly half of the company's stock. For another thing, the company can use all available means to encourage prodigious working hours. ("Even though I haven't had a vacation in thirteen years, and haven't had dinner at home in a long time, I still whistle on my way to work every morning," says one vice-president in the company described.) In recruiting for management, moreover, it can concentrate on finding the kind of man who is inclined to work this way; perhaps some kind of personality test will help for this purpose, or some indicator of on-the-job performance, or possibly it is necessary to apply the top executives' native intuition and have them do the interviewing. When promotions are made, the company can make sure only the hardest workers get them—and the same for salary increases.

When younger supervisors are coached and trained, the emphasis can be on inculcating the values of fast, top-level service and rapid decision-making. In corporate communications of all types, the focus can be on pride in growth, close customer contact, and personal stamina.

In such a manner would a company mobilize its human resources to carry out its strategy.

Moves and Countermoves

Suppose that after planning leaders survey the activities and behavior of key people, it appears that many of these individuals are acting at cross purposes with the program goals? Total mobilization then implies that one or a combination of steps must be taken.

TRANSFER OR REASSIGNMENT

It may be possible to transfer an individual to another department, division, or function in the organization. If, let us say, the plan calls for a large amount of risk-taking in investment and acquisition programs, and evaluations show that some of the decision-makers concerned are traditionally conservative or averse to taking the kinds of risks desired, these men may be transferred to another place in the corporation where their conservatism will not hurt the program. There may be positions in accounting, purchasing, or personnel administration, for instance, where unwillingness to gamble will do little damage to corporate aims.

To replace the managers taken out of the front line, individuals who do meet the desired specifications may be found in other departments and projects. When IBM moved ahead with its ambitious program for developing the System/360, Thomas Watson, Jr., and other top executives began putting more men with technical backgrounds into key positions; the power of marketing-minded men, who had traditionally reigned, was reduced. The reasoning behind this move was that, in meeting System/360 objectives, ability to master engineering and scientific problems and to direct talented subordinates in such endeavors was more crucial than IBM's well-established marketing genius. Some of the technical men advanced to the front line came from other functions in the company, and at least one of them had been the goat for another project that had earlier failed. IBM's top management trusted its knowledge of the man's capacities and did not depend on the record of his successes and failures. Companies that "inventory" their people in this way, viz., according to observed characteristics as well as win-or-lose performance, may (if their observations are perceptive) develop an enormously useful ability to shuffle individuals around in rapid response to changing needs.

DISMISSAL

Unlike IBM, which seems to prefer finding places somewhere else in the organization for "out" men (for instance General Products Division head John Haanstra, who was the leader of resistance to the System/360 concept, was not fired but reassigned to a less important project), some organizations would rather sever connections completely with individuals in key positions who are out of phase with the new strategy. They may reason that dismissal or the threat of dismissal is the best way of communicating rapidly to everyone the urgency of adopting new behavior patterns. As Michael Kami once said, fear is a superb communication device. A sense of security may be considered a fine thing for an individual so long as—and only so long as—it is tied to contributing to the desired outcome. "I saw the president of a subsidiary company change his whole attitude one day," reports James L. Hayes, "simply because the top brass said to him, 'This is where I want you to be, and if you can get there you can stay with the firm.' "[2]

[2] Quoted in Stewart Thompson, *How Companies Plan* (New York, American Management Association, 1962), pp. 101–102.

INCENTIVES TO CHANGE

In a number of organizations, management prefers the carrot to the stick in altering behavior. If individuals in a certain specialty or executive capacity are asked to take on more responsibility or activity, they may be given more power, better offices, larger budgets, or increased pay.

The efficacy of carrot-type incentives has been debated for years by social scientists and practicing managers, and even the most enthusiastic proponent is likely to agree that much depends on the individual concerned; for instance, the value placed on financial compensation varies with age, family need, training, and other personal factors. It seems clear, in any case, that incentives of this type are most effective if used in combination. When British Secretary of State for War Leslie Hore-Belisha was heroically seeking to modernize the British army late in the 1930's (see page 45), he decided that one means to the goal was making the service more attractive to young men as a career. Accordingly, he sought to place more stress on merit as the basis for promotion, on higher pay, on increased allowances, on better food, *and* on better barracks and living conditions. Hore-Belisha must have felt that no one of these improvements by itself would be influential, but that in combination they would dramatize the more attractive life of the career army man.

In a growing number of business and government organizations, executives are paying more attention to the possibilities of changing behavior by "job enrichment" or "job enlargement." They feel that if the manager or specialist is to think and act in new ways, the primary thrust must come from within him rather than from without; there is much he can do to change himself, it is believed, but he has only a limited tolerance for being changed by "the organization" through formal incentives, pressure, and threats. Frederick Herzberg of Case Western Reserve University and M. Scott Myers of Texas Instruments, Inc., are among the articulate spokesmen for this approach.

The planning leader has unusual advantages in employing the job-enrichment approach. The fact that his program calls for change means he is freer to create jobs as he would like them to be, rather than operate under the restraints of established custom. Also, he has a unique psychological asset to exploit: the bright goals of the plan, the hopes that the company has pinned on its accomplishment. By relating these goals to jobs and positions into which, as "architect," he has designed variety, scope, and challenge, he may be able in a short time to generate as much self-impetus for change as executives in charge of regular operations could produce in years.

One time the head of a new petrochemical company was talking to students at the Harvard Business School about the planning of his venture. He mentioned his success in staffing his organization with some of the finest young executives from the parent oil company. One of the students asked him how he had been able to do this. Had he offered large salaries and stock options? Yes, that had been part of it, he said, but it was not the most important thing because the "race horses" he had lured from the parent corporation had already been doing well in that regard. Most of them already had had Cadillacs and private planes. The really powerful incentive he had used was the goals of the plan itself. He had been able to offer his "race horses" key positions in a young company in which there would be lots of action, lots of variety, lots of excitement. Not only had this offering been a strong selling point, but it had also been a powerful means of encouraging his men to accept the long hours, large responsibilities, and entrepreneurial attitudes which he considered necessary to meet the long-range goals of the venture.

ALL MEN can see these tactics whereby I conquer, but what none can see is the strategy out of which victory is evolved.

—SUN TZU

PART III:

The Job of the Planning Leader

CHAPTER 10

The Need for Deep Involvement

ONE OF THE MOST pernicious notions about planning is that the job of the planner is to produce plans. "What is the output of a planning department?" a businessman once asked me. Answering the question himself, he said, "*It is plans and programs.*" In one form or another, this statement has been made countless times in the literature, at meetings of planners, and in discussions of planning. The idea underlies the job descriptions given numerous planners, the standards of performance they use, the assignments they accept, the methods they utilize. It probably arises from the natural tendency to equate "planning" with the work of certain planning departments in large organizations, when in reality more planning is often done by executives *outside* such departments than executives in them (the latter being restricted, in so many cases, to supplying and analyzing information).

Actually the job of the planner may have very little to do with the production of plans—at least, written plans (which is usually implied in the statements mentioned). In business, government, and education, some of the finest planning in this country has been done with no comprehensive written programs, no master planning documents, no "blueprints" of future action. Conversations, memoranda, meetings, reports, and actions—indeed, the planner may employ these, and in abundance—but no documents of twenty-five to two hundred pages plus charts, with neatly organized sections on goals, assumptions, alternative strategies, timetables, courses of action, and evaluation procedures, and with red, green, or black simulated leather covers.

To be sure, in a very large organization with a well-staffed planning department there may properly be in that department individuals who concentrate on the production of planning documents, forecasts, criteria, and similar matters. But these individuals, however capable or useful, are *specialists* or *advisers*. If we think of the planning executive in the more general sense—as an individual who is responsible for developing goals and/or for getting programs accomplished and who is as likely as not to have some operating responsibilities to carry out in addition to his planning—then it is an egregious mistake to equate planning with the production of programs. If, as indicated in chapter one, planning is a method of guiding and directing managers and employees so that their decisions and actions affect the future of the organization in a desired way, then the main job of the planning executive is to work with people to that end. This means getting involved in the problems people have in understanding planned goals and courses of action. It means getting involved in their problems of carrying out or implementing programs. It means hours and hours spent in explaining and listening and in persuading and teaching. If written programs with simulated-leather covers help toward this end, fine. But they may not. Very often in the past they have not.

Most planners and observers of business planning feel that the most important person in the process is the president or board chairman; whether a hero or a villain, he plays the lead role. The classic statement of the point comes from Myles L. Mace, who combines considerable firsthand experience in planning with research and teaching. He writes:

Effective corporate planning is not possible without the personal involvement and leadership of the chief operating executive. . . . Involvement and leadership mean spending the time and energy to manage the function—to see that something concrete is done. They mean personally putting into action what is too often abrogated by general words and phrases. In specific terms, there are two fundamental functions which absolutely demand the chief executive's active involvement:

(1) Leadership in the tough and laborious process of realistically evaluating existing product lines, markets, trends, and competitive positions in the future.

(2) Leadership in the establishment of corporate objectives.[1]

Similar statements might be made about the role of the head of a public agency or department, the president of a college, or the director of a voluntary health and welfare organization.

Obviously the head man cannot do all the planning by himself —at least, in an organization of medium or large size. In fact, one of the reasons it is so important for him to be involved in planning is that his actions get other executives involved in planning. In a truly planning-minded organization, the "futurity of present decisions," to use Peter Drucker's phrase, is as of much concern to key managers at the departmental, divisional, program management, work project, and similar levels as it is at the top of the hierarchy. When there is a sense of planning at these latter levels—when, in other words, planning influences employees' actions "where the rubber hits the road"—then, and not until them, can top management say it has done its job. "I am engaged in planning 12 hours a day, every day," the chief executive of a good-sized, fast-growing company once told an interviewer. "I don't know how you could run a business without thinking of the three- to five-year implications of everything you do today."[2] The head man who feels that way is usually the first to emphasize that his own sense of commitment must be great because that is the best way to spread planning-mindedness throughout the organization. The chief executive's office may be the place "where the buck stops," but it is where planning *starts*.

One of the great fiascos in the history of planning—Hitler's scheduled invasion of England in 1940—was due in part to failure to observe this principle. As writer Peter Fleming documents so

---

[1] "The President and Corporate Planning," *Harvard Business Review*, January–February 1965, p. 50.

[2] Thompson, *op. cit.*, p. 49.

well in *Operation Sea Lion*,[3] Directive Number 16, calling for the invasion of England, was issued by Hitler early in June. Later in the summer the invasion was scheduled for September 15; the code name for it was "Sea Lion." Although elaborate and very costly preparations for the invasion were made and although the "armada" was actually awaiting the word to depart from French and other ports on the scheduled date, the problems of successfully crossing and landing proved to be so great that the plans were canceled. A prime cause of failure was Hitler's lack of involvement in the operation. He delayed in giving Directive Number 16 in the first place; he wavered and delayed in giving orders necessary for implementing the operation swiftly; and, in general, as Fleming reports, "he took small interest in its planning." (Hitler kept hoping the British would capitulate or sue for a separate peace.) In consequence, the invasion preparations were hampered by bickering among commanders, numerous changes of plan, diversions of effort and attention to impractical schemes, and a multitude of last-minute difficulties that probably would have been taken care of earlier if the project had been executed better.

Making the Time Investment

Turning back now to more ordinary organizations and situations, let us look at the price of planning leadership in terms of time. How much time—actual clock time—does an effective planning executive spend on this work?

A formal study of this question was made by Phillip F. Myers as part of his doctoral project, mentioned in chapter one. Myers asked executives in six electronics companies, some of which were advanced in planning and some not, to estimate the amount of time they had spent during the preceding year on long-range planning. Any such question based on recall is, of course, subject to bias and other sources of error, and Myers did not claim his data were not thus "slanted." To reduce the error, however, he

3 New York, Simon and Schuster, 1957.

defined planning time as hours spent in management *meetings* devoted to planning questions; also, he was able to make some rough checks on the estimates. Hence his data have a fair measure of comparability, and as for the actual numbers themselves, the reader can adjust them up or down as he sees fit. Some of the highlights of Myers' study follow.

Myers addressed his question to executives at several different levels in the six companies and tabulated the answers separately. He began with chief executives. In three companies that had been doing planning with some success, as measured by changes in profits and sales as well as other indicators, the answers ranged from 500 hours to 1,000 hours (note that the latter figure would come close to half the president's time at the office). By contrast, in the company that had been doing most poorly in planning, the estimate was 30 hours. Talking to various subordinates in the firms, Myers heard such statements made as the following:

"Mr. Kellerdon [head of a notably successful company] not only feels strongly in favor of it, but he is the driving force behind it. In some cases he has stood alone in the face of short-term crises and has held out for long-range planning. He has pushed its implementation and holds it under his direction for that reason."

"From the impressions I've gotten from working with him [head of another successful firm in the study], he feels long-range planning is a necessary adjunct of management. He feels, and stressed just today in our meeting, the importance of the divisions making their plans very concrete and not general, so that he can follow them closely. He is a very enthusiastic backer. He was very involved in the early stages, but now has delegated the details. He does come in when the direction of the corporation is being set."

Myers then posed his question to lower-level executives in the six electronics firms. The median estimates of time spent in meetings on long-range planning during the preceding year were as follows:

For headquarters executives: 274 hours each (ranging from 500 hours in one very profitable company to only 10 in the firm that was the least successful of the six).

For division general managers: 208 hours each (ranging from 500 hours to 60).

For all top executives: 213 hours each (ranging from 350 hours in two firms to 30 in the least successful one).

On various occasions I have mentioned figures like these to businessmen and government officials interested in planning. Invariably a number of them react with dismay. Where is that kind of time for planning to come from? What about the other pressing matters which must be attended to by managers of dynamic organizations? In his book, *The Effective Executive*, Peter F. Drucker has provided a good number of insights into the problem of time management and offered a series of suggestions for handling it.[4] Here, in summary, are just a few of his ideas.

First, executives overestimate the importance of the activities they are doing and managing. "I have yet to see an executive, regardless of rank or station," writes Drucker, "who could not consign something like a quarter of the demands on his time to the wastepaper basket without anybody's noticing their disappearance."

Second, the key to improvement is time management, not activity management; that is, the place to begin is with a careful record (made *when* the events occur, not in retrospect) of exactly how the manager's time is allocated during a series of typical days in the office. His secretary is the logical one to make this record. "Time is the scarcest resource," Drucker notes, "and unless it is managed, nothing else can be managed."

There are always more activities and demands on a good manager's time than can be met. He could spend a lifetime managing these activities ever more efficiently and still not get around to freeing appropriate chunks of time for planning—*if* he insisted on attending to all important operating matters first.

Third, the manager should delegate all those things he does which others *could* do reasonably well. If he thinks of delegating only those matters that he does not consider "his" work, says Drucker, he will not delegate much at all (which is the reason

[4] New York, Harper & Row, 1966 and 1967. See esp. pp. 25–51.

the usual sermon on delegation does not cut much ice). Drucker adds:

> I have never seen an executive confronted with his time record who did not rapidly acquire the habit of pushing at other people everything that he need not do personally. The first look at the time record makes it abundantly clear that there just is not time enough to do the things the executive himself considers important, himself wants to do, and is himself committed to doing.

Recently *Forbes* held an interview with Donald Burnham, Westinghouse Electric Company's able chief executive. One of Burnham's answers, it seems to me, illustrates the foregoing idea. The interviewer asked Burnham how he managed to find time for the leadership activities he considered important, in view of the many demands on his time. Did he discipline himself by restricting the areas he got into? The answer was a firm *yes*. Burnham elaborated:

> For example, I don't sell our products. In some big companies with big orders (and in Westinghouse in the past), the president comes out and writes the order. I resolved not to do that. When the president starts selling, the customers won't deal with anyone but the top man. You get snarled up and your time is spent on that instead of thinking about the long-range planning.[5]

Fourth, productive work on high-priority activities (planning or operations) can be accomplished more efficiently if the fragments of time spent on the tasks are consolidated wherever possible:

> There are a good many ways of doing this. Some people, usually senior men, work at home one day a week; that is a particularly common method of time-consolidation for editors or research scientists. Other men schedule all the operating work—the meetings, reviews, problem-sessions, and so on—for two days a week, for example, Monday and Friday, and set aside the mornings of the remaining days for consistent, continuing work on major issues.

Drucker has little to say in favor of working home at night. "It enables an executive to avoid tackling his time and its manage-

[5] *Forbes*, April 1, 1968, p. 60.

ment during the day." (But he favors getting up earlier, from middle age on, to start the day earlier.)

Being Where the Action Is

Knowledge is one of the products of planning—but only one. Unfortunately, however, the knowledge outputs are often what catch the observer's eye to the exclusion of other outputs. He sees a dramatic forecast of change and growth, or a set of carefully spelled-out criteria for acquiring new companies, or a beautifully arranged PERT or critical-path diagram. "This," he says to himself, "is *the* product of planning."

But in planning, as every effective planner knows, the production of knowledge of what the organization should do and how it should act in the future is not the main or only job. In the first place, it is not just knowledge but knowledge *and action* which the planner wants to produce. Secondly, it is often not the production of knowledge so much as it is the crystallizing, clarifying, and unifying of what people in the organization *already* know that counts. And thirdly, in many cases it is not knowledge so much as *values* and *feelings* which matter in formulating and carrying out programs for change.

Because of this, what people often call the "leadership function" becomes crucial. Leadership in planning means much more than making decisions about plans. To emphasize a point made earlier, it means implementing decisions, following up on them, mustering support for them, revising them as necessary—in short, being where the action is. This is why great planners excel in the arts of communication, persuasion, "politicking," and organizing (all of which will be discussed in chapters to follow).

Nearly twelve centuries ago Charlemagne set an example in this regard which has been followed by effective planners ever since. During his forty-six years of rule, it will be remembered, Charlemagne sought to unify Christians in a peaceful kingdom and to reverse the trends toward moral and economic decay which were undermining European civilization. One of the outputs of his planning was knowledge. At the age of forty he hired a tutor (the remarkable Alcuin) so that he himself could learn science, language, philosophy, and art; and he hired teachers from abroad to instruct the younger generation in the various branches of knowledge. He demanded that the churches teach the multitudes. He promulgated new laws and standards. He imported works of art from other countries.

But Charlemagne did not let his planning stop here. It was not enough to produce the facts and ideas which outlined the peaceful kingdom he sought to create, though that in itself was a remarkable achievement. It was also necessary to make the plans a reality and, equally important, to bring reality into the planning. Charlemagne excelled at the latter, which was particularly important because his goals were so ambitious. From village to village he rode, tirelessly preaching hope in peace, listening to his subjects, seeking to administer justice, and endeavoring by his own example to inspire others to support his work. He had his lords report to him personally on conditions in their lands and on the moods of their subjects. He visited churches and bridges under construction, always trying to learn as well as teach. During the famine of 792, says the eminent historian, Harold Lamb, "He rode with despair in his heart through the land. His laughing presence gave strength to his weary people."[6] While hunting and swimming, he might quiz his companions relentlessly on their understanding of ideas and problems.

Some experts, no doubt, will object to such an example on the grounds that it illustrates not planning but the exercise of power or "kingship." It is true that, had Charlemagne no great design in mind, he might still have done many of the things described simply to bolster morale and strengthen the sources of his authority. But it is also true that he could not have been a great planner without acting as he did. What Charlemagne saw, heard, and did became extraordinarily important "inputs" into his plans; without his talks and tours he would have ended up building

[6] *Charlemagne* (Garden City, Doubleday & Company, Inc., 1954), p. 195.

castles in the air. What is more, his plans never would have been implemented if he had not been active in their support.

Planners today might ponder whether it is possible to be effective in a modern organization without following the same basic approach. If a business planner is not personally involved in management, so that he can use his personal "feel" of operations and people as "inputs" in his planning, can his plans be realistic? If a planner in a government agency is not personally involved in the implementation of new programs, can he convey his own understanding and inspiration effectively to others? An extraordinarily large number of planners—possibly even most of them, if noses were counted—have not bothered much about such questions or else assumed the answers were "yes." Perhaps it is high time to question that assumption.

"Ah," but some planners will say, "that may be so in implementational planning but not in grand strategy. In our organization our task is to concern ourselves with the major needs, threats, and opportunities, with the 'big picture' of what our management should be trying to do in the next five years. We leave the carrying out of plans to operating executives." This argument, too, seems to miss a major point. No "input" in strategic planning is more significant than the personalities of the key people who will be translating concepts into programs. How effective could a planner in Washington, D.C., have been during World War II if he devised Pacific theater strategy without an intimate knowledge of the personality of General Douglas MacArthur? MacArthur's age, his ideological conviction that the war in Asia was more important than the war in Europe, and his personal hostility toward his Commander-in-Chief, President Roosevelt, toward the glory-boy of the European theater, General Eisenhower, and toward the man whose career he had once sabotaged and who was now in charge (among other things) of matériels allocation to the Pacific theater, General Marshall—these and other elements of MacArthur's character bore as importantly on the realism of a strategy as did the numbers of ships, divisions, armaments, and supplies.

Once again, the planning of the Spanish Armada in 1588 offers a useful illustration. If Spain's King Philip II had understood his invasion commander better and revised his planning accordingly, the history of the Western World since then would have been different. During the last week in July, Medina Sidonia, commander of the invasion, had a superb opportunity to achieve his goal. His Armada lay off the southernmost tip of England, waiting for stragglers who had been blown off course during a severe storm. During that week the English defensive fleet, led by Drake and Howard, was in Plymouth Sound, where it had been forced by the storm. Medina Sidonia could have landed his fourteen thousand soldiers virtually unopposed, and in all likelihood they would have run only into minor interference on a march to London (the poorly trained English army was down to about two thousand men, the remainder having been sent to the Netherlands to help the Dutch defend against the Spanish). Instead, Medina Sidonia chose to stand off, get the stragglers, and proceed to Calais where he had planned to rendezvous with the Duke of Parma and to ferry the latter's forces across the Channel to England.[7]

The Spanish leader's timidity must have been due in part to his lack of naval and military experience. (In addition, he complained of seasickness and sniffles when he went to sea!) Also, he had not been in on the planning from the beginnning; the veteran Admiral Santa Cruz was originally slated to command the Armada, but Santa Cruz had died several months prior to the departure from Lisbon on May 9. Had he known Medina Sidonia better, Philip II surely could have used an approach employed successfully by many other planners: reviewing carefully all alternatives that might arise during the campaign and developing "decision rules" to be used, viz., agreements to depart from the master plan in a certain way or to turn to an alternative strategy. Lacking the understanding of a great planner, however, Philip

---

[7] For a superb account of the probabilities of victory at various stages of the invasion, see Walter R. Arnheim, "The Armada: An Operations Research Approach," *The MBA*, December, 1967, p. 19.

did not do this. In a number of ways, in fact, Philip appears to have been remote from the realities of his invasion scheme, laying strategy instead on the basis of military numbers collected in his office.

How does the great planner acquire sufficient insight about key people in the program? Mustafa Kemal, the master planner of modern Turkey, spent many a long night boozing it up with his political lieutenants; at another extreme, Alfred Sloan, the great architect of General Motors Corporation, made extraordinary use of factual evidence illuminating a subordinate's ability to get operating results, as well as of impressions gained in office conferences and golf played in knickers. The method does not matter so long as the result is veridical, viz., accurate and original information. I have found relatively few exceptions to this rule, and in those cases the planning leaders had unusually good second-hand sources of appraisal.

IF YOU do not think about the future, you cannot have one.
                                                    —JOHN GALSWORTHY

CHAPTER 11

Aggressive Communication

FOR MANY a public relations man, communication is a method of projecting an "image" of an organization or person, and the method is an artful one, full of tricks and subtleties. For the advertising copywriter, communication is the means to creating awareness of a product or service, and again it requires the deft and highly sensitive touch. For the negotiator of major contracts and "deals," too, communication is an occult art that only experts can master.

But for the planner, communication is none of these. It is a "nuts and bolts" part of his business. So long as he gets pertinent facts across clearly to the people concerned—the nature of goals and objectives sought, major assumptions, deadlines, assignments of responsibility, methods, and so forth—he has accomplished the job. He does not need to be clever or artistic, *but he does need to be aggressive.* He may have to repeat a message many times or go out of his way to make sure that the intended word gets passed to the right people.

In talks with managers in government, education, and business, I have heard the belief stated that it is not enough for top executives to be willing communicators themselves. Nor is it enough to encourage communication or even to create favorable conditions for it. These men are likely to indicate that in their opinion management should *direct* subordinates down the line to communicate—that it should *expect* them to be in touch with one another on pertinent matters. Otherwise, judgments that should be made will not be made or will be made by the wrong people. This attitude is characteristic of the energetic action-oriented manner with which planners, too, view this activity.

Few errors damage the human side of planning more than errors in communication. And the errors, interestingly enough, are almost always errors of omission, not technique of commission. Errors of omission seem to be due to two main causes: (1) the mistaken notion that to let others in "on the know" implies they must also share in the making of planning decisions; and (2) the feeling that one's knowledge of top-level plans should somehow be correlated with his rank and status in the hierarchy. The first notion is simply a misunderstanding; some highly dictatorial managements are also the most communicative. The second must be a vestige of times past when only "officers" were supposed to be able to think—and only fairly high-ranking officers at that!

Obviously there is no need to convey all of the information about a program to every manager and supervisor. Subject to that qualification, however, the nature of modern organization, whether in industry, government, or some other field, argues for generously communicating to a person or group the data which bear on its role in the program. Phillip F. Myers' interviews with lower-level managers in marketing, production, purchasing, and other functions provide elegant testimony on this point. Here are just a few samples of what he found:[1]

Contract negotiator: "In negotiating contracts [knowledge of corporate plans] gives me a much better feeling for how hard to go after a given contract. I'll take a worse deal on one, if I know that down the pike it will generate fallout or later projects and programs we want. I might go after the $5,000 study contract in a particular area we want to move into instead of a $500,000 production contract which is a dead end. Without long-range planning [by top management], I'd do my own personal planning, and it would not necessarily coincide with the company's."

Labor relations man: "If you're going to set up a new facility, you have to consider the implications. One year ago, one facility went

[1] The excerpts are from Myers' doctoral thesis, *op. cit.*

union. They chose a different union there than the one we gave in this facility [i.e., the speaker's plant]. If we had known a section of that plant was going to be moved here, we could have stopped that election. Now we have two different unions for the same kinds of employees, and we're going to have a jurisdictional dispute at the end of the contract. It easily could have been avoided with long-range planning."

Personnel executive: "Recruitment and training programs—we have to know what we're going to need in terms of machinists and model makers. You can't beg, borrow, or steal them. We're going to have to go into a large training program to produce these skills, and we wouldn't know it or do anything about it without long-range planning. We would live much more hand-to-mouth, work overtime."

Plant manager: "We're letting our plant go in terms of improvements, because we know we're going to have to move in 3–4 years. If we hadn't planned and didn't know this, we would probably put a fair amount into improvements, and then it would hit us that we had to move, and then we'd lose everything we put in."

Controller: "It [planning] helps me greatly personally. I always love challenges. . . . The company wants to grow and do a lot, and I want to be part of that and contribute. If they didn't have that, I would leave P.D.Q. If the President had plans to double everything, but didn't tell anyone, I would start looking at the want ads. . . .

"I'm working on a consignment program for inventories, and I wouldn't be able to evaluate the program without planning [and knowledge of the aspects that affect me]. I can sell the supplier on going along because I know what we are going to be doing. This gives you the lowest possible price. Otherwise, if I couldn't tell him what our needs were going to be, he would laugh at me."

Salesman: "Every salesman has his own built-in plan. He is out meeting people in various ways for future sales. I'm going out and cultivating medical people now, because I think we're going to be moving in that direction. My knowledge of planning has helped me point our sales agents in the same effective way toward likely future prospects."

A friend of mine who is with a large appliance manufacturer tells me that communication of top management's plans is similarly important for overseas personnel, especially those who are engaged in buying foreign companies, plants, and facilities. Unless these negotiators are aware of planning decisions, he says, they make blind-alley analyses that later prove to be fruitless, have to do considerable backtracking and reversing of positions taken, and find themselves doing too many jobs on an expensive "crash" basis—all of which piles up needless expense. He quoted one executive as remarking: "The deadly enemy of a negotiator or strategic planner is *surprise* regarding any implicit policy or reaction of top management which he did not know of or anticipate."

As the foregoing examples suggest, aggressive communication is vital because there are so many action centers in modern organizations. An unfortunate legacy of the past is the commonly held picture of organization as a pyramid, with thinkers, decision-makers, and order-givers at the top and "sergeants and soldiers" the rest of the way down. To be sure, grand strategy may be reserved to some narrow area at the top, but a better picture of a modern organization would be a large area of interlinking circles of assorted shapes and sizes, each representing a center of discretion, initiative, and action. To be sure, this picture would be more true of organizations employing new techniques and technologies than organizations that do not, and more true of change-oriented organizations than static ones—but do not such types increasingly typify the current scene?

Admittedly, a risk goes with generous communication of the content of plans. The information may leak to a competitor (in the case of business) or to a nonfriendly power (in the case of the military). Without meaning to minimize these risks, for they may be real indeed, one may well ask this question: Has the risk of a leak been realistically weighed against the risk of inaction or ineffective action due to employees not understanding the parts of the plan which bear on their work?

Keeping the Right Goals in Focus

In almost every sizable organization whose leaders have ambitious plans, a continual conflict goes on between top management and middle-management bureaucracy. The details vary, but whether the organization is the Soviet government under Stalin[2] or an American corporation, the basic plot is the same: the aims of planning leaders for the enterprise as a whole are at odds with the aims of departmental and division heads for their functions. In other words, there is a tug of war between the total and the parts—or, to use the social scientist's wording, between the group and the "subgroup." If the scene is an American corporation, the sales manager of Division A may be more concerned about the status, security, and internal politics of the Division A sales department than about the corporate-wide goals for profitability and diversification which are uppermost in the minds of executives at headquarters—and the two may often be in conflict. If the scene is Russia under Stalin, the heads of the NKVD may be more concerned about their private rivalry for power with the Red army than with the Kremlin's long-range goals for dominating Eastern Europe—and these two also may be in frequent conflict. The essential plot of group versus subgroup is practically universal; only the personalities and details vary.

This friction is a major threat: if not held in check, it makes the central planner impotent. It should not be surprising, therefore, that planning leaders make tireless use of communication to show—and keep showing—the needs of the enterprise *as a whole* to the men and women who direct its individual parts. In presentations of long-range plans, in budget documents, in memoranda, in speeches, in personal discussion—in these and other ways the planning executive keeps reminding division managers and project heads of how their actions affect the overall result.

It may be helpful to conceptualize this matter. Two social scientists, Tom Burns and G. M. Stalker, have devised the terms "mechanistic" system and "organic" system. The former applies to the organization in which the parts think as separate units; the latter, to the organization in which the parts think as mem-

[2] See, for example, Merle Fainsod, *How Russia Is Ruled* (Cambridge, Harvard University Press, 1963); cited in Gerald Sirkin, *The Visible Hand: The Fundamentals of Economic Planning* (New York, McGraw-Hill Book Co., 1968), p. 60.

bers of a whole. (As for analogies, the human body is a good example of an organic system, while an example of a mechanistic system might be a quaint old colonial house in New England which has had new rooms, wings, and rooflines added one by one over the years.) As Burns and Stalker describe the mechanistic system, drawing on their studies of a series of Scottish and English firms, it poses severe problems for planners. The authors state:

> Each individual pursues his task as something distinct from the real tasks of the concern as a whole, as if it were the subject of a sub-contract. "Somebody at the top" is responsible for seeing to its relevance. The technical methods, duties, and powers attached to each functional role are precisely defined. Interaction within management tends to be vertical, i.e., between superior and subordinate.[3]

The authors' study shows the mechanistic firm to be capable enough of operating under stable conditions, but not able to respond effectively to needs to change. This is because it responds by means of an adding-on approach. If the times appear to demand that the firm adopt a more aggressive marketing program, a sales forecasting and market study group will be *added on;* if a more aggressive research and development program seems to be demanded, a new development team will be recruited and *added on;* and so on. But the rest of the firm goes on operating as in the past. As it does so, employees in the old departments will view the new group as a threat, resist it, and fight it in behind-the-scenes maneuvers—but they will not change their ways because the new requirement on the enterprise is for those in top management to meet somehow, not for the people in the old departments.

What about the organic system? Here the picture is different. All of the divisions and departments in the firm adjust to accommodate the change. Job descriptions change a little, groups work together in slightly different ways, managers and other employees alter the way they approach their tasks. Also, Burns and Stalker find, jobs get done by people at the same level agree-

---

[3] *The Management of Innovation* (London, Social Science Paperbacks–Tavistock Publications, 1961), p. 5.

ing to work together in new ways, without forcing top executives to decide whether and how a change should be made. "Interaction runs laterally as much as vertically."

Not surprisingly, this yeastier type of organization, with many more centers of initiative, more problem solving, and a fairly blurred organization chart, is characterized by more controversy, tension, and uncertainty in employees' minds than is the mechanistic system. But its tension is the tension of creativity, of an organization "on the move." The study demonstrates clearly that the organic system adapts and responds far more effectively to changes in the economy. Instead of a market study group being added on, as with the mechanistic system, a marketing orientation is cultivated throughout the existing departments, making a new function unnecessary; instead of a new research specialty being added, the present engineering group itself cultivates the new skills and facilities needed, with supporting changes as needed from purchasing, manufacturing, and personnel specialists. (In each case, of course, internal personnel shifts may be made, too, and new people hired if necessary, etc.)

In terms of cost and efficiency, to say nothing of the general spirit of employees, the organic system is obviously superior. And from a planning standpoint, its advantages are virtually priceless. This is because planned changes become part of the warp and woof of the organization in an organic system; they become "internalized." So it is no wonder that great planners are seen exploiting communication in every way possible so as to foster organic systems instead of mechanistic systems.

The Great Trade-Off

There is a basic philosophical conflict between planning and certain other functions. Without doubt, a liberal, relatively wide-open policy of divulging planning information makes for a less closely knit, less exclusive management elite (in addition to the risks of undesired "leaks" to outsiders). What is more, the stress placed on planned goals of the whole enterprise instead of on individual departmental goals tends to break down neat boundaries of authority and chain-of-command patterns.

To some people, such costs are intolerable. They provoke, Burns and Stalker report, "an urge for the clarity, the no-nonsense atmosphere of a mechanistic organization." Lost is the ability to divide a task quickly into parcels, to know exactly who is accountable to whom, to realize immediately how to proceed because past practice can be repeated, to be able to feel unquestioningly secure. Burns and Stalker asked employees in the organic companies to explain the structure of top management. "In no two cases did there appear to be agreement on who constituted the stratum of management under the head trio." Moreover, "no one at the top was quite sure how he stood relative to others; of whether one person's ascendancy was permanent or temporary; whether something which needed doing should be done by himself, another, or someone else." In the organic systems employees everywhere possessed more anxieties and felt more embarrassments (although they also felt more dependent on each other and more committed to each other).

Such is the price of a planning-oriented communication strategy. Is it worth the gain of rapid adaptability to change, of a thoroughly coordinated quest for planned goals, of an organization in which new ideas are contagious and one part can quickly infect another with a fresh viewpoint? Sometimes the answer is dictated by economic necessity—as when the enterprise must either plan aggressively or die. But more often management has a choice. That choice depends on leaders' values, on their "gut feel," as well as on rationalization.

Not all organizations have to lead in planning. Not all organizations must aggressively seek to fill changing public needs. Not all organizations have to possess a "sense of mission." Nor do all need to keep changing and adapting internally. If policy-making executives feel their companies, colleges, governmental agencies, or other organizations can get along without changing and leading, they may find it logical also to reject the kind of communication program necessary to support entrepreneurial planning. However, if they do *not* feel that way but believe wholeheartedly in entrepreneurial planning, then the costs referred to will seem quite modest in view of the gains to be achieved. There will be no doubt in their minds how to make the trade-off.

For a fateful example of communication tactics, let us turn again to Hitler's planned invasion of England during the summer of 1940. The project required a high degree of coordination and cooperation between the army, navy, and air force—precisely interlocked schedules as well as much mutual support. Such coordination, in turn, demanded excellent communication between the services. Hitler, as the planning leader, was in a position to initiate and generate such communication—but he did not. In fact, he purposefully prevented it at the top level. For instance, he made it a point to talk with his commanders-in-chief individually; only once during the summer of 1940 did he see them together, and that was on September 14, just before the invasion was put off (the operation was to have begun on September 15). Hitler's preference for tête-à-tête talks was due to his fear that if he dealt with his top commanders as a triumvirate, they might combine to oppose him. He could manipulate them better on a man-to-man basis.[4]

Thus, Hitler chose the risk of poor coordination in planning rather than the risk of losing some personal control. On this particular occasion, at least, his choice was an extremely costly one for the Nazis. The risk materialized, poor coordination led to extra delays and failures, and the plan came a cropper.

WHATEVER course you have chosen for yourself, it will not be a chore but an adventure if you bring to it a sense of the glory of striving—if your sights are set far above the merely secure and mediocre.

—DAVID SARNOFF

[4] See Fleming, *op. cit.*, p. 53.

CHAPTER 12

The Unhidden Persuader

ONE OF THE GREAT PLANNERS of the past fifty years is Turkey's Mustafa Kemal, or Ataturk. By some standards, Kemal would be considered a maverick planner because he never wrote out a master plan, nor did he crank into his national development programs such standard inputs as forecasts of gross national product or of demographic movements. Instead, he kept his master plans in his head and taught them verbally to subordinates, and his forecasts were of popular reaction and response rather than economic factors. He understood the human side of planning well and exploited his understanding. In at least one vital respect, he was unequaled.

To appreciate this skill of Kemal's, we must recall first that he worked in the face of enormous obstacles and subject to continuous hindrances and irritations—the ingrained sense of tradition and resistance to change in the Turkish population of the 1920's, a lack of strong managerial reserves, a cloud of personal scandals (generally of the amorous type), several breakdowns of his health, and other problems. Yet in the space of about a decade he wrought a social, political, and economic revolution in Turkey the likes of which the world has seldom seen. After abolishing the sultanate in 1922, this man who had previously been only a military hero drafted a constitution for the new Republic of Turkey in 1923 and became its first president. In 1924 he abolished the official hold of the Moslem religion over schools and other affairs. He went on to scrap the holy law, mystical societies, the fez, and (in 1928) arabic script—all part of the traditional warp and woof of Turkish society. He emancipated women, freeing them to go about town without veils, to dance in public, vote, exercise legal rights in divorce suits, and enter government. He introduced land reform.

These and other features of Kemal's revolution were all part of a mosaic of change which he had in mind at the outset. More than that, the parts of the mosaic tended to reinforce one another, thus producing the kind of synergistic effect described in chapter 9 (and which, we pointed out, few planners achieve). How did he pull it off? Almost invariably he developed popular support as a first step, then proceeded to push his reforms through the legislative machinery (much of which, of course, he controlled). But how did he persuade the people—a population which, to repeat, had no tradition of receptiveness to change?

When he started his campaign or "subplan" to abolish the fez, he had himself photographed on a tractor wearing a panama hat instead of the traditional garb. He visited the most reactionary villages first with his panama hat, not the more progressively inclined towns. When campaigning for the emancipation of women, he arranged gala balls in the cities and started things off himself by dancing with a woman. He appeared before the people over and over again to give speeches about modernization—again using the shock treatment, in many cases, by delivering his talks first at the conservative strongholds. In addition, he was not above using fear as a method; the "hanging dictator," as he was sometimes called, executed a good number of political enemies.[1]

Kemal taught planners of all types—in industry and education as well as government—an important lesson about selling a program. In these times when the term "hidden persuader" is part of our lingo, his lesson is a refreshing one. It is that planning rests on *un*hidden persuasion. Far from being a behind-the-scenes manipulator, the planning leader must be obvious and conspicuous—the more so, the better. People down the line need to see the paraphernalia and prestige of his office behind his

[1] For a fine account of Kemal's life, see Lord Kinross, *Ataturk* (New York, William Morrow and Company, 1965).

efforts to change their thinking. His "visibility" is one of his priceless advantages. If he does not lend it to the program, no one else can.

After making a study of many efforts by corporations to carry out important changes in the behavior and practices of employees, some of these efforts successful and some unsuccessful, Larry E. Greiner found that the cases of success were almost always characterized by a high degree of involvement on the part of executives introducing the changes, whereas this was not so in the cases of failure.[2] For instance, those who effectively commenced and carried out sweeping changes spent a considerable amount of time in face-to-face, give-and-take sessions with subordinate managers, lower-level supervisors, hourly workers, and union representatives. Why was such involvement important to success? One of several reasons, Greiner found, was that the personal participation of leaders was clear evidence to employees everywhere that top management valued change and was willing to face up to the problems of change—its own problems as well as other people's. Without such involvement and commitment, "it is doubtful that lower levels *can see the need* for change or, if they do, be willing to take the risks that such change entails" [italics added].

Unlike the organizations that failed in their attempts to change, Greiner added, companies that succeeded were managed by men who did not try to delegate the job of involvement and persuasion. Although the delegated approach was appealing because of its "democratic" connotations, Greiner speculated that it "may remove the power structure from direct involvement in a process that calls for its strong guidance and active support."

How They Do It

Watch the day-to-day behavior of men and women who make and carry out major plans effectively—and who make the neces-

[2] Greiner, *op. cit.*, p. 119.

sary adjustments in the plans so they *can* be carried out—and you will detect an underlying principle of persuasion. Contrary to popular myth, it is not a trick of manipulating minds or a gimmick of "psychology." Nor does it conceal, in the *general* run of cases, a threat of demotion or retaliation, for, as some teachers are fond of pointing out to students who would solve a problem by firing everybody who throws up resistance, there soon would be no one left to manage if dismissal were the cure. Rather, this principle is a fairly simple one. It is that the person to be persuaded usually has not one but several viewpoints that affect his attitude toward a change. (Behavioral scientists may refer to these viewpoints as "self-concepts.") Often these views will be somewhat inconsistent with one another. By making the person aware of any such inconsistencies and by stressing the viewpoint that would lead him to support the change, the persuader can succeed in "selling" him. Let us turn to some examples.

Suppose a marketing program calls for several men who were formerly sales managers to become marketing directors instead, i.e., assume responsibilities for supervising a variety of selling activities, without becoming involved in the daily operating details of any one. Now suppose—as so often happens—that the sales managers have trouble making the transition. They have got used to thinking of themselves primarily as salesmen—as the men who bring in the orders. And they have come to take great pride in their mastery of the mystique of salesmanship. Now they feel threatened by the prospect of letting subordinates become the "stars" in selling, even though there is more pay and authority in a marketing director's job.

How does the planning leader deal with such resistance? He has little chance of changing the men's concepts of themselves as star salesmen; concepts like that may be in the grain for life. However, he will see if he can play on *other* self-concepts and needs that the men have—concepts that may indeed be more consistent with the new program. For instance, they probably think of themselves as loyal, dedicated, "company-first" men. The leader can work on that feeling, pointing out that if the men want to put the company first in action as well as thought, they will strive to find satisfaction in helping their subordinates become sales stars and not be jealous. He will say, in effect, "It's wonderful to be a great salesman, and I understand your pride in that, but you also are proud of your loyalty to this company and we need you as a marketing director. You cannot be that and a salesman, too."

If most employees affected by planning had neat, simple, logical sets of values and self-concepts, the planning leader would have to close up shop. Fortunately, most people have unusual and often illogical mixtures of ideas. It is this fact that gives the planner his chance to sell individuals on planned change. Commonly, therefore, the first step he takes is to make the individual aware that his reason for resisting a change conflicts with some other idea he cherishes. Or better still, before the individual can display resistance, the planning leader will begin bringing out those of his values and self-concepts which are likely to make the program seem appealing to him.

In his case study of change in a retail chain, Paul Lawrence finds:

> Changed organizational expectations, as signaled by changes in structure and personnel, will, by definition, put many people in the organization into a conflict position as regards their established self-concepts. There is no way of escaping this conflict. It seems, in fact, to be a necessary prelude to effecting any real change in behavior. The evidence of this study indicates that making the conflict clear-cut is a necessary first step for resolving the conflict. By making their new expectations clear-cut, management can highlight this personal conflict. This step can be difficult because some tend to deny the existence of the conflict.[3]

Lawrence also finds that this step *alone* is not always sufficient; it may have to be reinforced by other incentives, pressures, and management actions.

Behavioral scientists often refer to a person who tries to pro-

---

[3] *The Changing of Organizational Behavior Patterns, op. cit.,* p. 195.

duce new attitudes among organization personnel as a "change agent." By this definition, all planning leaders as we think of them in this book are change agents. An interesting example of a change agent in action is given by Paul Brouwer of Rohrer, Hibler & Replogle, the well-known firm of industrial psychologists and consultants in Cleveland:

A vice president of sales was brought in from outside the company to gear up the effort of merchandising a new line of products. He did a magnificent job, old pro that he was, of shaping up and vitalizing a sales force. Volume of sales picked up excellently, and he was the hero of the hour.

But after a year, when he felt on top of his job, some of his attitudes and habits reasserted themselves, annoying others and stalling progress. For instance, he persisted in making frequent references to his former (and larger) company. He climbed on manufacturing for delivery delays, and on research and engineering for perfectionism before releasing the specifications for what he felt were needed product changes. The time it took to explain to him, pacify him, and argue with him was ill-spent and futile. He was rapidly becoming a block in the path of progress.

One day the president approached him directly. "George," said the president, "what's your title?"

"Why," said George, puzzled, "vice president of sales."

"Right. And what does vice president mean to you?"

George paused. What was the president getting at? "Well," he said, "it means a lot of things, I guess. Responsibility for sales, building a . . ."

"Stop right there," interrupted the president. "Responsibility for sales, you say. True in a way. But the sales manager also has this responsibility, doesn't he?"

"Well, yes."

"Then what does the word *vice president* mean in your title?"

"Oh, I see. . . . Well I guess it means seeing or having responsibility for the sales function of the company from the point of view of the company . . . that part of your office."

"You got my point before I mentioned it, George," said the president. "A vice president speaks from the company point of view, not just his department. He tries to keep the overall good of the company in mind."

George thought this conversation over. He got the point. He realized the narrowness of his own view. He had been thinking of himself as "on loan" from his former employer to straighten things out here. As he pondered the president's comments, he broadened his perception of his job—and of himself. And sometime later he began to act as an officer of the total company.[4]

To emphasize the idea with which we began this chapter, the planning leader is a conspicuous persuader. Whether dramatizing his new expectations, as Mustafa Kemal did, or probing an individual's or group's thinking for attitudes that he can use and perhaps making apparent to them conflicts of attitude, he operates visibly, in person. Kemal knew that Turks were hidebound by tradition. He also knew they yearned for a better life, that they had heard of modernization in the rest of the world and felt uneasy about being left behind. He knew they felt great pride as individuals and a people. When he appeared with a panama hat instead of a fez, when he opened a ball by dancing with a woman, when he personally inspected the new plots of land owned by farmers—in such ways he appealed to these latter desires and values. "You love your traditions, but you also desire emancipation," he said, in effect. "The two are in conflict now. If you want emancipation, you must go along with me. All the powers of my office will be with you."

Letting Questions Do the Work

On a rainy afternoon in April, 1863, General "Stonewall" Jackson walked slowly along the bank of the Rappahannock River where the Confederate army was camped. He studied the river, tried to make out the terrain on the opposite side where the Union army was stationed, and pictured what it would be like to cross the river and advance on the Federal dispositions. That was what he wanted to do, what he had been impatient to do ever since morning. But all day he had been haunted by Lee's question: Wouldn't it be better to wait for the enemy to attack,

---

[4] "The Power to See Ourselves," *Harvard Business Review*, November–December, 1964, p. 163.

if that was his plan? To a soldier of Jackson's inclinations, it was an almost irresistible temptation to strike at an enemy who was hugging a riverbank; properly executed, and with some luck, such a strike could be enormously successful. But a large risk was involved, too; four months earlier on another battleground, on the evening of December 13, Jackson's advancing batteries had paid dearly for taking that risk. Lee was asking him now, why not let the Federals assume the risk? Jackson pored over his maps, pondered the ranges, gun positions, and ground to be covered. "At length and most regretfully," reports historian Douglas Southall Freeman, "he had to own to himself that an advance would be costly and that withdrawal would have to be under devastating fire."[5]

Part of Robert E. Lee's genius as a military planner was his ability to ask his lieutenants discerning tactical questions *and leave it to them to get the answers.* "If you think it can be done," Lee told Jackson on that rainy day in April, "I will give orders for it." Thus Lee helped to develop a sense of responsibility, study, and commitment on the part of his famous lieutenant. But note the implications of such an approach: the senior planner's personal notion of what the plan should be must frequently be altered. If the subordinate feels the "question" is really a conclusion, he will not bother himself to make a pointless study. So while the planning leader takes on himself the responsibility of seeing that planning done, he entrusts much of the *substance* of program development to his lieutenants.

In the example just given, the questions had to do with short-range tactics. It is not infrequently stated that good leaders may leave "tactical" answers to their juniors, but reserve questions of a "strategic" or "policy-making" nature strictly for themselves. Experience does not bear out this generality. I worked with one fine planner who threw out the question, "What kind of organization scheme should we have in five years?" and expected the answers to be formulated by the managers. Another fine planner

[5] *Lee's Lieutenants: A Study in Command* (New York, Charles Scribner's Sons, 1944), II, 526–527.

I know once created quite a stir in his organization by asking executives, "Where do you want to be in five years?" The thinking thus precipitated may have centered at first around personal career planning, but in a short time it led also to fresh thinking about formal divisional and departmental programs. When Robert McNamara became Secretary of Defense under President John F. Kennedy, he wrote up and circulated for Pentagon officials a long list of policy questions. "McNamara's 76 trombones," as the questions were called, stirred the atmosphere and helped prepare for the basic, far-reaching changes that the Defense Secretary put into effect.

Once again, the planning leader is a conspicuous persuader. He does not ask questions surreptitiously or delegate the asking of them to a trusted subordinate. He asks them bluntly, frankly, in person. He puts the prestige and authority of his office behind them. "I want you to plan," he says, in effect. In this case he adds, "You do not have to take my ideas for the plan, but it is important that you produce ideas you will stand behind." To persuade a sales manager to get involved in planning, he might ask such questions as:

Are the needs of your customers changing, and if so, how?
Would we do better if we put most of our effort on different types of customers or on different territories?
What about new kinds of selling effort—e.g., team selling?

To persuade a production head to become more planning minded, he might ask such questions as:

What are your plans in case your quality control expert resigns? What would you do if your maintenance specialist leaves?
One of our perennial problems is inventory. What are other companies doing in inventory management? Are they doing things to improve forecasting that might be helpful here, or are they experimenting with field warehousing or combinations of air freight and regional center location that might have possibilities for our operation?
How could your department improve its coordination with the research division or with the marketing department?

A college dean might ask of a department head:

What teachers will you be counting on most five years from now?

What trends are occurring that may change the subject matter your people are teaching or the manner in which they teach it?

Should your teachers be taking special courses to update their skills and knowledge?

The Importance of Being Dramatic

Even with all of his prominence and prestige, the planning leader faces many difficult tasks of persuasion. He is likely to lay his hands on any aid, tool, or trick that he thinks may be helpful. One such aid is dramatization. Not surprisingly, most of the great planners have used it repeatedly. In their hands, of course, dramatization is not the tool that it is in an artist's hands—but on occasions it may be almost as important.

How does a planning leader dramatize a program? He may use handsome visual displays of programs—charts and maps that will help his audience more readily visualize the tasks and relationships involved. In these days the displays may be tied in with computational facilities so that a chart can be changed within moments to show the effect of a different assumption or condition. Some United States corporations have well-equipped rooms for the discussion of plans and programs; DuPont's chart room is the best-known one. Perhaps the most famous facility is that used by top military planners in the Pentagon. Defense Secretary Robert McNamara saw the need for dramatization soon after he took over the Department of Defense in 1961. He had his office of programming design a room with four Vu-graph type projectors that displayed against four adjacent screens. On one side of the room a tramrail was installed to bring forward chart data for an approved program on floor-to-ceiling posters. On the opposite side of the room a tramrail displayed other posters showing specific elements of the program that were under examination. The decision-makers sat in the center of the room. A computer that contained the charting and display data was located behind the projectors. It was alleged by the Department of Defense that if a planner asked a question regarding a trade-off in resource allocation (e.g., how would costs change if Defense built so many more landing and take-off bases instead of having so many new carriers), the question could be run through the computer and the answer charted and projected on the screen in seven minutes time![6]

Simulation has similar advantages as a tool for dramatization. The leaders of one well-known company consider their efforts at financial simulation—that is, using a computer to project the combined effects over time of hundreds of possible conditions on the company's cash flow, earnings per share, and reserves—to be far more significant than certain laboriously prepared written programs. The reason is that simulation is a kind of "live" demonstrator. Any assumption, condition, or expectation can be changed quickly and its effects on planned goals seen almost immediately (whereas the lengthy document would have to be sent back to the planning department for rewriting).

A quite different tool is fear. Early in this chapter we saw how Kemal used fear to dramatize his dictatorial powers in planning. In the ordinary situation, fear is created by firing a lieutenant who fails, or by conspicuously demoting or humiliating him. Disagreeable as it may be in the minds of many people, fear can nevertheless be a potent medium.

Note that all such forms of dramatization possess a common element—demonstration. Demonstration is made easier by modern visual and computational techniques, but it by no means requires them. Nearly twenty-two centuries ago one of the first great military planners, Hannibal, used a simple, crude technique of dramatization with enormous success. In 218 B.C., after his army had left Spain, crossed the Alps into Italy, and begun its southward advance on Rome, Hannibal's task was to recruit able and eager fighters from the local Gauls and Celts. Accomplishment

[6] Donald J. Smalter, in a talk to the College of Planning, Institute of Management Sciences, New York, May, 1964.

of his long-range objectives would be out of the question if he could not bolster his manpower continuously. Hannibal himself understood clearly the power of incentives; by pledging freedom (as well as riches) to conscripts, he knew he could meet the need. But he could not do the job all by himself; he must persuade his whole army to join with him in the task. One evening in camp on the plains of northern Italy, he staged a fight between two captured slaves. To the victor who killed his foe Hannibal promised freedom and equality with the Carthaginians in his army. Although the combatants were weary and hungry, they fought with astounding ferocity and intensity (even with allowance for their survival instincts). Hannnibal's officers and men got the point of the demonstration and worked together with great effectiveness to recruit soldiers in the campaigns that followed.[7]

There is nothing so easy but that it becomes difficult when you do it with reluctance.

—TERENCE

[7] Harold Lamb, *Hannibal: One Man Against Rome* (New York, Doubleday & Company, Inc., 1958).

CHAPTER 13

Politics for Planners

POWER AND "POLITICS" play a very crucial role in planning. Whoever the top planning executives are, they are the target of political intrigue and "power plays" engineered by other leaders and would-be leaders. Indeed, such goings-on may affect planning even more than other leadership functions, because so many managers and employees tend to regard planning as a personal threat. Also, they may *think* that planning is expendable, even if it is not in fact. Unlike executives in, say, marketing and finance, the planning leader cannot count on tradition and long acceptance to establish the need for his presence. Therefore, whether he is spending part or nearly all of his time on planning activities, he must tend his political fences assiduously or risk losing his influence over others.

"Some people feel it is in bad taste to talk about power in a business context, but it is one of the facts of business life," states Robert N. McMurry, Chicago's well-known industrial psychologist who has probed deeply into the workings of countless companies. "A corporate executive uses power to get things done. This, of itself, does not make him evil or sinister—power is neutral: neither good nor bad—it merely makes him a true manager."[1] The statement applies to officials in education, government, and other fields as well as business. And Antony Jay points out: "Real power does not lie in documents and memos

[1] *McMurry's Management Clinic* (New York, Simon and Schuster, 1960), p. 140.

outlining your terms of reference and area of jurisdiction: it lies in what you can achieve in practice. . . . Power lies in the acceptance of your authority by others, their knowledge that if they try to resist you they will fail and you will succeed."[2] Of course, no one has unlimited power, not even in dictatorships.

McMurry lists ten "tricks of the trade" for chief executives anxious to survive in organizational politics:

1. Use caution in taking counsel.
2. Build as many limited alliances as possible.
3. Maintain maneuverability.
4. Use passive resistance when necessary.
5. Limit what you communicate.
6. Be willing to compromise on small matters.
7. Use self-dramatization.
8. Radiate self-confidence.
9. Avoid being too close to your subordinates.
10. Be ruthless when necessary.[3]

Jay gives seven "positive guiding rules" for maintaining executive power in an organization:

1. Always take the heaviest responsibility yourself.
2. Remember that your own craft skill is not a rampart for your defense but a barrier to your advance.
3. Always hunt for the disquieting evidence.
4. Spend most of your time among the most powerful group in the organization.
5. Win opposition over to your side or at least to neutrality; don't raise your own private army to fight it.
6. Remember that thought is a prelude, and not an alternative, to action.
7. Look for problems through a telescope, not a microscope.[4]

All such rules that apply to executives in general apply to planning leaders. But which rules of "politicking" have especial significance for planning heads? And what additional rules would they be well advised to follow because of the peculiar nature of their work? These are the questions we shall examine in this

---

[2] *Management and Machiavelli* (New York, Holt, Rinehart and Winston, 1967), p. 139.
[3] *Op. cit.*, pp. 143–145.
[4] *Op. cit.*, pp. 145–146.

chapter, drawing for counsel on a wide variety of experiences. As will readily be seen, this discussion is applicable primarily to those in planning who wield decision-making power. Many of the rules to follow have only peripheral interest for those individuals, committees, and departments that are limited to specialized functions, such as supplying financial data for top management or gathering information on divisional programs.

1. The head of planning must command the respect of other leaders in the organization.

One leading corporation took a high-level executive who, though well liked, had lost the professional respect of his colleagues and kicked him upstairs to be head of the planning committee. By so doing, management hoped to restore him as a key member of the team; instead, it put him in an impossible situation and failed to get much mileage out of planning. To compound the error, the company appointed to the ranks of the committee not top management people but men at the department head or assistant vice-presidential levels who could not possess or gain all the information they needed to draw up effective programs. Not surprisingly, the company's vice-presidents resented having their subordinates doing such potentially important work. "Although I do not think they openly sabotaged the efforts of this planning committee," reports Edward Scheu, then a member of this company's management, "they did not openly support it either. They rather looked down their noses at the whole operation. They seemed to say: 'Well, you boys do all this fancy planning; then we will go out and buy another mill and that will destroy all your plans.' "[5]

The amount of informal authority and respect possessed by a planning executive depends in considerable part, of course, on his skill in playing the rest of the political game to be described. But however he gains it, the fact of his having it—and the official support of top management, too—has a crucial bearing on his

[5] "The Management of Planning," in Dan H. Fenn, Jr. (ed.), *Managing America's Economic Explosion* (New York, McGraw-Hill Book Company, Inc., 1961), p. 124.

ability to succeed. Respect is not the same thing, it must be emphasized, as popularity. This distinction is fortunate because the planning function is often a threat to the peace of mind of other departments in the organization (especially in the early stages of planning), and a planning leader who tries too hard to be well liked may soon render himself impotent.

2. *Know who stands to gain and lose from proposed plans and programs.*

In nearly every case of successful planning, the executive in charge had a mental balance sheet of who would be helped or hurt by a new program. More likely than not, he acquired this intelligence during the formulation of the program rather than during its implementation so that he could profit from the information when working out strategies and tactics.

Let us suppose that the planner seeks to introduce "systems purchasing," viz., an arrangement under which an outside supplier takes on the job of monitoring the corporate buyer's need, keeping adequate inventories of the goods under contract, and assuring immediate delivery as required. On the planner's mental balance sheet of gainers and losers from the proposal, he would probably count marketing men as gainers (since they would presumably gain a price advantage from systems purchasing); on the liability side of his ledger, however, he would probably have to count the people currently employed in warehousing and inventory, for their jobs in the company would be threatened. Also on his balance sheet, listed perhaps as contingent gainers or losers, he would want to count the key people to whom marketing, warehousing, and inventory employees report or with whom they have informal alliances, for these key people are likely to be influenced by the claims of the prospective gainers or losers.

At a meeting of professional planners I once attended, one of the men mentioned the great value of weekly planning meetings that were held in his company. The meetings brought planning and operating people together. At the sessions, planners could often sense who were the potential resisters of proposed changes.

"You have to know this," he emphasized, "and you won't find it out from memoranda and telephone calls."

3. *Maintain working alliances with other departments and functions.*

Working alliances are not only protective but invaluable as channels of comunication, as McMurry observes. He warns against making them too strong, however, for the ally may fall from power or prove to be disappointing later on. We might add that a variety of limited alliances is preferable to one or two. The planner can keep his ear to the ground better if he has working pacts with a number of departments, and he is not then likely to become suspect of perennially promoting one group at the expense of another.

The planner has natural bases for limited alliances with many groups in a business corporation, university, or government agency. For instance, by shaping his programs with a view to the interests of financial executives and communicating pertinent data to them, he can help them borrow funds at optimum rates and plan more effectively for adequate cash flows in the future. Working in the same way with personnel managers, he can help them anticipate future needs for recruiting and training employees so they will not be caught at the last minute with having to start "crash" programs. In return, both finance and personnel can give the planner valuable support not only in gaining management approval to go ahead with a program but also in implementing it.

4. *Allocate most of the time you spend in discussion and contact work to the power centers of the organization.*

In short, do not let yourself become heavily engaged with pricing experts, market analysts, programmers, or other staff specialists, or with operating people at middle or lower levels. Emphasize your contacts and appearances with key executives.

In one sense, this rule is a fairly pure form of management

snobbery. Taken too seriously, it can cause considerable resentment among managers and specialists who get snubbed for lack of "rank"—and these people can return to haunt the planner some day if they rise in influence, as they often do. On the other hand, the planner is well advised to recognize that "this is the way life is" and that he had best act accordingly if he wants to be effective. What is more, there is an intellectual justification for consorting mainly with the key policy- and decision-makers: *their* judgments, attitudes, and values, more than anyone else's, are basic inputs to a major program. These subtle elements are not likely to be found neatly spelled out in some document; they must be sensed in their ceaselessly varying, evolving, perplexing, and sometimes contradictory forms. This assessment cannot be done unless the planner is physically present with the executive in question, able to observe his gestures, tones of voice, and responses to different questions and problems.

5. Try to make yourself indispensable to nonplanners.

Operating people often complain that planners have blind spots in their appreciation of workaday operations. At the same time, people engrossed in everyday operations have blind spots, too —and the latter can be very dangerous. The accounting manager in the 1950's who was overly engrossed in making his traditional operations more efficient risked being put out of business by the rise of electronic data processing, and the manufacturing vice-president who too successfully resisted model changes suggested by marketing men took a grave risk of finding himself with no orders at all as customers switched to other producers. Drawing on his continuing studies of developing trends and opportunities, the planner can save nonplanners from the dangers of their blind spots.

Jay gives the example of the Duke of Wellington in 1810 (but uses the illustration for a different point).[6] Wellington's army was fighting one of Napoleon's forces in Portugal. Although quite successful for a period, Wellington found it necessary to with-

[6] *Op. cit.*, p. 184.

draw from one area and retreat toward Lisbon. With the French in close pursuit, the British began to lose their hope and enthusiasm. On the tenth day of their retreat they came to the mountains of Torres Vedras. What they saw there came as a complete and wonderful surprise. Ready for them to use immediately was a superb network of trenches, forts, palisades, and other positions, complete with guns in position and dammed-up marshes to trap any attacking foe. These defenses, says Jay, must have taken a year to build; Wellington had foreseen the need for them long before. One can well imagine the impression he must have made on the "day-to-day" thinkers on his staff. By virtue of his planning ability, he had truly made himself indispensable.

6. Keep the toughest jobs for yourself.

Many people are glad to think of themselves as planners in a limited sense; that is, they have pet ideas about the future, major opportunities, and their own potential importance in the scheme of things to come. Even though they do not concentrate on such general notions with the professional attention of a planner, these people may not concede him any superiority of insight, understanding, or clairvoyance. This tendency is a source of chronic irritation to many planners, for the implication is they have no special expertise.

Generally speaking, the planner might just as well resign himself to this state of affairs. There is, however, one way that he can assert himself. A sizable share of the planning job is likely to consist of difficult, arduous tasks; he can make these jobs his unassailable domain. Foremost among such tasks is the professional, painstaking collection and assimilation of information about the human implications of organizational plans and programs. But this is by no means all. For instance, in the case of questions of choice between alternative courses of action, each of which has its advantages and disadvantages—what are often called "trade-offs"—it may be the planner who has to make the firm recommendation that will surely bring down on him the wrath of the defeated protagonist and to defend that recommendation repeatedly with facts and figures. In the case of long-term financial forecasts, it may be the planner who has to work out the pro forma profit-and-loss statements under different and tricky assumptions for a series of future years—again a job that may consume as many long hours in defense and review of the figures as are required by the initial preparation itself. In the case of analysis of future strategies, it may be the planner who, toiling with computer experts, programmers, and operations researchers, has to "run with" the mathematical model and simulate the effects of different actions and conditions. In the case of multi-division companies, it may be the planner who has to find a way to put different divisional programs together, making them dovetail financially as well as in terms of marketing, manpower, and other requirements. Where there are lengthy presentations to be made to executive committees or boards of directors, it is again the planner, of course, who probably has to work out the presentations of slides, maps, and graphs and be ready to answer scores of difficult questions ranging from methodology to fundamental assumptions.

Such time-consuming jobs are not so likely to be coveted by anyone else. Willing acceptance of them by the planner gives him a trump card that few will want to challenge. His mastery of of these tasks will give a little more pause to those who would usurp his power or emasculate his budget.

Jay cites the Roman Emperor Augustus as an example of a political leader who strengthened his position by keeping difficult tasks. Augustus maintained personal command of the most troublesome provinces in the Roman Empire because "he knew that if he delegated to someone else the responsibility for the toughest job in the empire, and authority over the biggest army in the empire, he might be creating an even greater problem than he was solving."[7] At the opposite extreme, Shakespeare's King Lear is the classic example. Lear delegated complete authority to his daughters Goneril and Regan. He was then shocked and chagrined when they turned him out of their castles, dis-

[7] *Op. cit.*, p. 140.

missed his bodyguard, and left him desolate. One cannot have both power and freedom from responsibility.

7. *Keep your commitments, positions, and programs flexible.*

"You wouldn't think much of a poker player who took one look at the deal and then announced exactly what he planned to do," says McMurry. "Business and poker have much in common; they require decisions based upon incomplete and possibly inaccurate information."[8]

Idealists register disappointment when they see veteran planners following loose-jointed and often fragmentary programs of change. The idealist would like to see an inspiring master blueprint; when he observes the veteran pursuing a one-thing-at-a-time course, he may react with some such words as "That's hardly planning." What he fails to appreciate is that the planning leader loses part of his freedom to negotiate and maneuver once he commits himself to a comprehensive, fully detailed program of action. That loss may be fatal in the political give-and-take that so frequently characterizes organizational leadership. Moreover, promulgating a detailed blueprint of action means that little room is left for others to make proposals to advance the cause along. One of the most politically effective tactics a planner can use is to wait until other executives come forth with an idea for moving in the desired direction, then swing his support to them so that *they* acquire the prestige that goes with originality and innovation. And by supporting them, he gives them cause to back him when *he* needs help on a proposal—the kind of log-rolling game that legislators play, only with different stakes.

In a McKinsey Award–winning article, H. Edward Wrapp, a one-time corporate planner who is now director of the executive program in the University of Chicago's Graduate School of Business, comments as follows on the case for flexibility:

The public and the stockholders, to be sure, must perceive the organization as having a well-defined set of objectives and a clear sense of direction. But in reality the good top manager is seldom so

---

[8] *Op. cit.*, p. 143.

certain of the direction which should be taken. Better than anyone else, he senses the many, many threats to his company—threats which lie in the economy, in the actions of competitors, and, not least, within his organization. . . .

Subordinates who keep pressing for more precise objectives are in truth working against their own best interests. Each time the objectives are stated more specifically, a subordinate's range of possibilities for operating are reduced. The narrower field means less room to roam and to accommodate the flow of ideas coming up from his part of the organization.[9]

Of course, there are occasions when the need for swift and comprehensive action is so great that it is worth the risk of promulgating a detailed master plan. When this is the case, the planner can protect himself in two ways: (1) spelling out the assumptions on which a course of action is based so that if unexpected conditions develop, he can invite discussion of changed programs without discrediting his efforts that went into the original plan; (2) laying out alternative courses of action that the organization can take if the selected route leads to unanticipated difficulties. Both of these devices keep the planner out of a straitjacket, preserving some opportunity for him to maneuver if his political alliances in the organization change or if unexpected opposition develops to a program and threatens his power.

8. *Support continuous change in the procedures and policies followed by the organization.*

As Wrapp points out, the successful manager is likely to be seen espousing new proposals and ideas even if the current strategy seems to be producing fine results. One reason is that he is an opportunist; only with "many changes in the works," as Wrapp says, can he seize on the combination of ideas here and there which in his opinion will best keep the organization growing.

This approach is particularly important in the political life of a planner. If, as we have said, he must keep his alliances flexible,

[9] "Good Managers Don't Make Policy Decisions," *Harvard Business Review*, September–October, 1967, pp. 94–95.

if he needs to keep himself indispensable to nonplanners, if he needs to maintain limited commitments to programs and goals so that he can maneuver and alter his position—then he must have a continuing stream of opportunities for changing his tactics. There will be such a stream if the organization never gets set in its ways but keeps evolving and mutating.

The planner can help to assure such an atmosphere by his enthusiasm for other executives' proposals, by tactful questioning of the status quo, by the way he goes to others and seeks to draw out their knowledge and experience. If it would be in his interest to have the company broaden its product line, the "excuse" he needs to start the wheels working in that direction may come from a distribution manager's proposal for a new study of customer shopping patterns. "I'm with you," the planner says. "You can count on my support. And let's be sure we ask some questions about other products people wish they could get from us." (Actually the distribution man was thinking of the need for a larger warehouse, but he's glad to expand the scope of his study in exchange for the planning executive's support.) Or perhaps the idea the planner is looking for comes from someone in the finance department who hears of a small company whose owner-manager might like to sell out. The financial man thinks of the beneficial effect of the acquisition on the company's price-earnings ratio. He worries, though, about the fact that the other firm produces a product that is "out of our present line." The planner assures him that should not be an obstacle. "It looks like a fine buy to me, too," he says. "And maybe it wouldn't be such a bad idea if we did get in some other markets."

These are the *kinds* of workday opportunities that the planner feeds on in order to strengthen his working relationships with other departments and increase the perceived need for his services. The point is that such opportunities will not arise unless the right "climate" exists in the organization—a climate of active interest in change. Although the planner cannot create that climate by himself, he can help to create it by giving all the encouragement he can to those who have new ideas and suggestions regarding the way things could be done.

*9. Compromise on the less important matters when something can
   be gained thereby.*

In 1862, Otto von Bismarck, who was working to unite the
Germanic states, met a brilliant socialist, Ferdinand Lassalle. Lassalle, one of the great Jews of that period, was an intellectual
leader of what was then considered "socialism"; he advocated
improved working conditions for factory employees, old-age
pensions, cooperatives, profit sharing, arbitration in labor dis-
putes, life insurance societies for workers, advance notice to a
worker to be discharged, and other measures. Bismarck, at the
time Premier and Minister for Foreign Affairs for Prussia, had
little real sympathy for Lassalle's socialism; in fact, Bismarck rather
detested most of the philosophy—as he did middle-class idealism in general and authentic constitutionalism. Yet he threw the
power of his office behind Lassalle's program.[10]

Why did Bismarck do this? Lassalle had strong popular support
but was short on political weapons; Bismarck had the political
weapons but needed more popular support. By allying himself
with Lassalle, Bismarck mustered the additional popular strength
he needed to advance his programs to create a strong united
Germany. This latter goal, in his mind, was far more important
than his distaste for Lassalle's ideas. So the man whom historians
have called the first state socialist in Prussia was actually one who
disliked the philosophy as much as many other Prussians did.

Bismarck's compromise was much greater and more personal
than that which the planner is usually called on to make (and, of
course, of far greater importance historically). Yet it drama-
tizes the enormous value of give-and-take in the political contests
that go on in organizations. In a large percentage of the cases,
the planner is simply practicing what might be called "coexistence." He knows that a division sales target could and should
be a little higher, but the difference is not crucial to him and so
he acquiesces to a lower figure because this enables him to stay
on good terms with the division manager; in exchange, he wins

[10] See Emil Ludwig, *Bismarck* (Boston, Little, Brown and Company,
1927).

the acquiescence of the division manager to a proposal that truly *is* vital to the planner.

One of the most interesting forms of "coexistence" has to do with unplanned or unauthorized innovations in departments like research, engineering, and marketing. Strictly speaking (and this is the way we generally see or hear it advocated), once a program is formulated and approved by management, there should be no departures from it until an official revision is made. Otherwise, say the "purists" and disciplinarians, the organization's limited resources will be dissipated, top management has only partial control, and the chances of success for the program are reduced. In theory they may be right, but in practice there are other considerations to weigh. The precious spirit of spontaneity and inventiveness, for instance, may rise in conflict with a plan of action—and that spirit, too, is important to preserve. The politically wise planner, therefore, does not seek to control too tightly. Using his judgment, he permits a certain amount of "bootlegging" and diversions of energy (especially when the promoters are willing to do most of the work on their own time). With a little luck, the organization will be repaid many times over for his tolerance. The initial creative work that led to IBM's development of the memory disk for computers was done by a technical group which "bootlegged" the work when it could not get official budgetary approval; and the initial investments of time and energy which led to Lockheed Aircraft's important ventures into systems analysis for hospitals and medical clinics were made by employees who kept working on their pet project despite many early rejections from management officials.

An additional value of a coexistence policy is that it stimulates the general climate of change in an organization. As pointed out earlier, such a climate is politically expedient for the planning leader.

10. *Don't raise "private armies" to fight the groups that oppose you.*

When the politically wise planner finds himself at odds with other factions in the organization, he tries to persuade the opposition to come to his side or, at least, to become neutral. Consistent with his belief in "peaceful coexistence," earlier described, he avoids internecine warfare if he possibly can (although he may be an eager warrior in the competition with other organizations in the field).

One of history's fine examples of this policy is William the Conquerer. William, it will be remembered, determined to invade England when Harold was crowned king in January, 1066. He claimed he was the appointed successor to his cousin, Edward the Confessor, who had been the king before Harold. William's bid for wide support for his planned invasion began auspiciously; the Pope gave him his blessing and proclaimed him to be Edward's rightful successor. But when William approached a number of barons in Normandy and asked for their support, they were evasive. They said he should convene a larger assembly of Normans. William did that, asked the collected barons to support his invasion scheme, but was again turned down. They would serve him in Normandy, they said, but not in the invasion of another kingdom, with all of the dangers involved.

At this point, William the "Planner" (as he might well be called) must have been tempted to fight the barons into submission. He could have mustered the support of bishops, abbots, merchants, knights, other rulers, and some of the more sympathetic barons, and sought to overpower the dissidents. Instead, William sought further to persuade. He approached the barons individually, beginning with the richest and most powerful of them. In private conversations with them, he said they were not obligated to support him but he would consider it a personal favor if they would do so. He promised to cut them in on the treasures of victory (he was good to his word after the invasion); he offered them written guarantees "sealed with his great seal." One after another they agreed to support him, pledging large amounts of money, ships, and other resources.[11]

[11] See George Slocombe, *William the Conqueror* (New York, G. P. Putnam's Sons, 1959), pp. 113–118.

11. Sometimes you will have to be ruthless.

There are degrees of ruthlessness, and usually the less severe degrees will suffice—but not always. In this respect the planning leader is no better off than any other executive who seeks to maintain his power.

In one case, ruthlessness took a comparatively mild form. The heads of a business firm were trying to get long-range planning started, and after several abortive starts they decided to arrange a weekend think-in at a retreat in the country. It so happened that the particular weekend in question was a nearly impossible one for the firm's manufacturing head; to join in the planning session, he would have to be absent from a family function that meant a great deal to him personally (and to his wife and children). He explained this eloquently to the executive vice-president, who was in charge of arrangements. "You don't have to come," the executive vice-president told him, "but we will go on and make our plans without you." This meant, as both men knew, that the interests of manufacturing might be jeopardized by certain other men at the session. The manufacturing executive came to the think-in—probably at the price of an unfortunate family crisis.

In another case, the form of ruthlessness was more drastic. The planning department of a company was at loggerheads with the president. The planners placed almost all of their emphasis on the criterion of maximum profitability, while the president was inclined frequently to compromise profits in favor of furthering national or international causes that he considered worthy. Although the planning head was accountable only to the president and had no business reporting information to anyone else, he knew there were members of the board of directors who were on his side. But to make their move at a formal meeting, these directors needed certain information he had given the president. The planner went "over the president's head," gave copies of the data to the board group, and had the satisfaction of seeing the president ousted from his job.

12. *Communicate selectively.*

This rule may seem somewhat in conflict with our notes on the need for open, generous communication (chapter 11). And it is. Here, as elsewhere, expediency may argue for a slightly different course of action than do the simple facts of what operating people need to do a good job. I do not think the effective planner accepts one of these views *or* the other. Rather, he recognizes both and judges when one is more essential and when the other.

McMurry, from whom this rule is adapted, warns against communicating information "which might create unnecessary anxiety or schisms in the organization." Such information arises most frequently of all, it seems, in the planning process, and that is one reason that the rule has especial relevance for planners. They are the ones who are most likely to see ominous clouds on the horizon. And they are the ones most likely to begin devising plans for change which will affect the security and status of many managers and other employees. If they were to talk freely about their problems and ideas, there is no telling what emotional trauma they might create, much of it needless. This would not help them stay powerful and effective. Also, it might greatly restrict their freedom to maneuver. Hence the successful planner is often found holding back information for a while, although ideally he might like to communicate it.

For example, suppose that plans are being formulated for a new marketing venture. The program has important implications for the personnel manager; he will have to get some new kinds of training programs under way, revise some job descriptions and perhaps salary ranges, and work out other measures. The more lead time he can be given in starting on such projects, the better. Nevertheless, the planner holds back from the personnel director information about the venture under consideration. For so long as questions about the timing, scope, and direction of the venture remain, the planner will be freer to change his position—to make special accommodations, let us say, for several powerful executives he wants to please—if he has not said anything to the personnel director and started that person making plans of his own for implementing the new program.

"By using care in determining who learns what, and when, you will enhance your ability to maneuver," says McMurry. "Remember, though, if something is bound to leak out, it ought to come from you and bear your interpretation."[12]

13. Don't get too close to your subordinates.

This rule (also an adaptation of one of McMurry's) is especially pertinent to planning—and in particular the head of a planning department or task force. For one thing, he needs continually to keep the "people aspects" of planning in perspective with the physical and material aspects. Never an easy task, this will become inordinately difficult if he allows himself to become beholden to any of the specialists working for him, whether they are operations researchers, forecasters, or some other variety. Should he become thus beholden, he will lose credibility in his dealings with other subordinates.

What is more, in his relations with the rest of the organization the planner is continually under suspicion (as emphasized earlier) of being impractical, removed from operating realities, detached from the workaday urgencies of getting results. He will find it harder to minimize this suspicion if he is seen as being too close to his own subordinates. If their personal feelings seem to be the basis for his decisions and if he does not appear to be a boss who can say no to them, then he operates under a cloud in his relations with nonplanners.

14. Keep alert to unpleasant problems and troublesome trends.

Jay's fourth rule is "Always hunt for the disquieting evidence," and his seventh rule, "Look for problems through a telescope, not a microscope." Unlike many employees in purely operating jobs, the planning leader has a vested interest, one might say, in discovering needs to change. If there appears to be permanent stability in the field in which the organization operates or if there

[12] Op. cit., p. 144.

are no developing weaknesses in the organization's position vis-à-vis other organizations in the field, then the *raison d'être* for planning is not easy to explain. Furthermore, many employees preoccupied with daily operations would like to *think* they can continue unmolested in their present ways even if that is not the case in reality. One of the planner's jobs is to wake them up to warning signs of change and to shoot holes in the status quo.

Watchfulness is equally important with respect to internal problems in the organization. Are rifts between units developing which may jeopardize the execution of a program? What subtle shifts in human values and attitudes are occurring which will influence the kinds of goals and policies people will work enthusiastically for? Where are there possibilities of a program being sabotaged because of antagonism toward planning? The planning leader who is not well informed on questions like these is like a poker player betting on hole cards he has not looked at. What Wrapp observes about successful executives he has known applies with especial force to the planner:

> As he moves up the ladder, he develops a network of information sources in many different departments. He cultivates these sources and keeps them open no matter how high he climbs in the organization. When the need arises, he bypasses the lines on the organization chart to seek more than one version of a situation.[13]

15. If possible, create vested interests in your programs among outsiders.

This last rule is not always applicable to planning situations, but where it is, it enables the planner to put an extra string in his bow. If receptivity to and interest in a new program can be developed among outside leaders and groups with whom the organization does business, then more pressure can be brought to bear on potential rivals and opponents of the program.

During the 1930's in the United States, TVA planners had to contend with widespread opposition to the idea of government going into the electric utility business. The fact that the TVA became, as George Soule has remarked, "the most striking single

[13] *Op. cit.*, p. 92.

success of the New Deal."[14] is due in no small part to the allies it was able to win in the communities where it did business. The architects of this new agency saw to it that not only would consumers in the Tennessee Valley gain by virtue of cheaper and more plentiful electric power, but so would local governments and even privately owned utilities. Local governments gained because TVA planned to (and did) give them the equivalent of the taxes the agency would have paid if it were private. Privately owned utility distributing companies gained because, while their prices for resale of electricity were held to a low maximum by TVA, the demand for such power was so great they made higher profits than before.

Robert Woodruff, the head of Coca-Cola for many years and an able planner (*Forbes* called him "one of the most remarkable men in recent U.S. business history"), used a similar technique in implementing his company's great expansion plans between 1923 and World War II. "We want everybody who has anything to do with this company to make money," Woodruff said.[15] One strategic outside group was the pharmacists. He had schools set up for them where they could learn, at Coca-Cola's expense, how to run a successful pharmacy—how to sell more aspirin, lipstick, cough drops, Vaseline, and so forth, as well as more Coke. Woodruff knew that if pharmacists could succeed in bringing more people into their stores to buy lipstick or toothpaste, more would stop at the soda fountain on their way out to have a Coke. One can readily imagine the value of such outside alliances to Woodruff whenever he sought to sell his organization on ambitious new targets for sales volume and supporting facilities.

A WISE executive once told me: "Anybody can plan five years ahead, but it takes real management skill to leap from crisis to crisis."
—MICHAEL J. KAMI

[14] *Op. cit.*, p. 129.
[15] *Forbes*, August 1, 1967, p. 27.

CHAPTER 14

Organizing
To Get the Job Done

ONE OF THE SUREST WAYS to separate the amateurs from the professionals in planning is to compare their attitudes toward organization. The amateur is likely to rely on enthusiasm and zeal to get planning work done. He insists that planning (with the exception of such occult forms as mathematical programming and PERT) can be done by everyone who really wants to do it and that the leader's job is therefore to inspire and motivate, to spread the seeds of desire throughout his staff. He contends that spontaneity, which is extremely important in this business, can be stultified by organization charts, boards, committees, channels, and the rest.

The professional does not deny that much planning can be done on the basis of motivation alone, nor does he minimize the importance of spreading inspiration and desire. But he thinks of organization as a means of furthering and developing these qualities, not retarding them. He points out that almost the entire history of planning makes an airtight case for good organization, showing very few cases in which it was not present in the planning of major programs that succeeded and equally few cases in which its absence was not followed by failure.

As for spontaneity, the professional planner values it no less highly than the amateur does. But organization—and management methodology in general—is not the enemy of spontaneity but its ally, the professional says. Organization is one of the planning leader's means for multiplying the opportunities for people to collaborate and strike creative "sparks." As George F. F. Lombard once observed in the course of making a broader generalization from case studies, an administrator's skill is "by management to *improve* the chances for spontaneity" [italics added].[1]

Varieties of Assistance

A long-familiar question in the literature is: Should planning be done by line or staff executives? The question has been debated repeatedly by learned men and women. Ironically, it is the wrong one to ask. Planning should *always* be done by line executives. The real question is: How much and what kind of help, if any, does the line need in planning? On the answer to this question hangs the decision whether or not to employ planning specialists. There may or may not be a need for special skills of analysis or extra manpower and brainpower to carry out assignments, and these skills and "bodies" may or may not be needed for more than a limited time. Considerations like these are the decisive ones.

(The planning-by-line-or-staff question breaks down for another reason, which is that in modern organizations it is often extremely difficult to make neat distinctions between "line" and "staff." As we have rephrased the question here, the distinction no longer matters.)

RELYING ON THE LINE

The leaders of some successful organizations feel strongly opposed to letting planning be done by anyone other than policy-making executives in charge of operations. The very idea of employing a "director of corporate planning," viz., a person removed from operating responsibilities, in order to develop new programs for the line organization to follow is anathema to

[1] *Behavior in a Selling Group* (Boston, Harvard Business School Division of Research, 1955), p. 341.

them. "It would mean one man interfering with another," said a corporate executive at Time, Inc., in early 1967. Another Time executive, the publisher of one of the divisions, said:

My own job is more than 50% planning. We did appoint a Director of Planning once, but it didn't work and after 18 months the post was abandoned. In any case, I want planning to be the warp and woof of what we do, so we are all doing planning. I want everyone thinking about the future. . . . Evoking brilliant new thinking should come through regular dialogue and I want to do it; it's my job—it's the top executive's job. And if there's to be any "rational delegation" to be done it should be delegation of *operations*.[2]

The chairman, editor-in-chief, president, and executive vice-president at Time, Inc., stated that they had a form of "multi-management" in which each kept the others informed of anything important going on, could substitute for one another, and could be allowed to take several months off when necessary to study a problem affecting the future. "We four plan, really," said the chairman. "Sometimes we meet at 6:00 P.M. and don't finish talking until 11 o'clock . . . talking about what sort of a company we should be in the future."[3] (As we shall see later, however, Time employed a group of specialists for one phase of the planning job.)

In organizations that effectively rely on operating people to do the lion's share of the planning, how does the executive keep his subordinates involved in the work so that they do not succumb to the forces of antiplanning earlier described?

1. He sets a deadline for the first step. If this is not done, there is too good a chance that the first stage of a planning task will be postponed and repostponed under the pressure of other deadlines. Moreover, when it is difficult to work out a complete program at the outset because of changes and uncertainties, completion of the first clearly needed step often clarifies what must be done next.

2. He asks that the best available figures be used even if they are suspect. A popular excuse for postponing planning is that certain information is not clear or verifiable. The effective plan-

---

[2] Time, Incorporated, a case copyrighted in 1967 by the President and Fellows of Harvard College (ICH 12C14, BC 290, Harvard Business School), p. 13.

[3] *Ibid.*, p. 5.

ner is not swayed by this excuse. He says, in effect, "Well, let's use the best data we have and see what happens." If it turns out that the data are completely erroneous, some time, work, and money will have been lost, but at least planning will have got under way. More likely, though, the data can be "firmed up" and revised as the work progresses without having to start all over again.

3. Often he encourages subordinates to set their own targets and to decide how they will achieve objectives. The target will, of course, be what academicians call "subgoals," viz., intermediate or subordinate goals. (Decisions about the end goals always should be made by the heads of the organization.) While exceptions to this practice are justified on many occasions, it is based on sound psychology. For one thing, the target a bright, capable person sets for himself may well be more ambitious than what his boss would set for him. Also, a person feels more committed to a goal or method he chooses himself than to one his boss sets for him. In addition, the person is likely to choose the ways and means which happen to suit him best.

Such advantages were once described by William C. Treuhaft, President of Tremco Manufacturing Company:

We say, "Mr. Sales Manager, we'll give you all the resources, the money you need if you justify it in your plan. We have the money, and we can give you what you need. But you have got to figure out how you are going to achieve the goal that has been set for your division, and what you need to enable you to achieve it." Some managers are inclined to say, when the performance of their unit is not up to the goal, "Well, you pulled that goal out of a hat. I'm doing the best I can, and I think I'm doing a good job. Look what I did last year. If I don't reach that objective, it isn't my fault."

We are inclined to answer by saying, "This is your goal. It is reasonable. When we set it up first, you thought it was reasonable. But regardless of that fact, we are confident, based upon knowledge we have of other organizations, that this amount of growth is attainable. It is your job to tell us what you need to do it. If we can't give you the resources you need, then you have a legitimate out, but not otherwise."[4]

[4] See Thompson, *op. cit.*, p. 104.

FULL-TIME PLANNING DEPARTMENT

Unlike the heads of Time, Inc., many chief executives feel the need for a formal planning department whose primary function is to help operating managers draw up plans and/or make plans itself for their approval. In small, single-product, or centralized companies the aides will work in a headquarters office; in decentralized or multi-product companies they are more likely to be attached to the different operating units and work with the local managers (in which case they may report also to a corporate director of planning who works with one or two assistants at headquarters). In government and education the pattern is less clear.

The full-time planning department is becoming ever more popular in industry. It has been estimated that the number of such departments has been doubling every three years since the late 1950's,[5] and in education, government, and other fields the same trend is in evidence, although at a slower rate. While part of this increase must be attributable to faddism, a substantial portion must reflect increasing satisfaction with the potentials of a separate planning unit. Then, too, organization heads seem to be developing more sophistication about the proper role of such a unit—in particular, that it should advise, help, and prod operating managers in their planning and see to it that sufficient planning is being done, but carefully avoid any attempt to take over the responsibility or act as the judge of a program drawn up by a department or division. Some years ago the vice-president of central planning for Swissair was commenting on the patience required of planning specialists cast in this role. He said, "It is people who must put plans into effect, and while it is comparatively easy to specify an aircraft it takes much longer to 'specify' people. Recognition of this, and patience in letting people accept ideas and develop their own may be the most important continuing challenge for the Planning Department."[6]

[5] Richard F. Vancil, "So You're Going to Have a Planning Department!" *Harvard Business Review*, May–June, 1967, p. 88.
[6] Swissair ©, a case copyrighted in 1960 by l'Institut pour l'Etude des Methodes de Direction de l'Enterprise (IMEDE), Lausanne, Switzerland.

Where the planning department is an effective working part of the organization, it is almost always seen to be "using" top executives as well as being "used" by them. That is, it carefully ascertains how executives feel about key elements of a program—for instance, the amount of risk that can be taken, the likelihood of major changes in demand, debt capacity, and what new facilities can be built or acquired—before it undertakes a major study, and during the course of a study it will check back with chief executives when an important question or policy-making matter arises.

Edmund P. Learned, serving with the United States Air Staff during World War II while on leave of absence from the Harvard Business School faculty, noted that much staff work was wasted because the generals did not keep on top of it as the work progressed. Learned found that staff officers would often go ahead on a project and complete it before turning the results over to the commanding general. In the meantime, of course, one or more staff officers would have become committed to the recommendations and analysis. Hence the general could not substantially revise or alter the report without hurting the committed staff people. If, on the other hand, he had kept on top of the staff work, following its progress and giving his judgments on critical questions along the way, this would not have happened. He would not then have found himself in positions in which the staff officers, in effect, were making his decisions for him.

A second generalization that can be made about planning departments that have successfully fitted into the management picture is that they vary enormously in approach, scope, size, "personality," and almost every other aspect. In one of his reports on a detailed study of planning department operations in business, Richard F. Vancil cast his findings in the style of a magazine column by the eminent pediatrician, Dr. Spock. Thus, Vancil offered some counsel on the treatment of illnesses contracted by the "child," i.e., the planning department. He wrote:

> Like any growing child, planning departments are prone to catch a wide variety of childhood diseases, most of them not very serious and easily cured, but some of them occasionally fatal.

The minor illnesses, remarkably similar to the mild epidemics of measles or mumps that spread through an elementary school, occur most frequently right after the head planner has returned home from a "Seminar on Planning Techniques." There he has been exposed to a wide range of esoteric notions about why planning works so well in everybody else's corporation, and, not yet having developed a natural immunity to such ideas, he succumbs to the "bug" and tries to apply the new technique at home. The problem, of course, is that elaborate procedures for, say, planning research activities may be vital to a pharmaceutical company but of much less importance to an appliance manufacturer.

The simplest cure for such maladies is to allow them to run their course. Other members of the family should be sympathetic but, being older and wiser, should refuse to cooperate in spreading the disease through the rest of the corporation. Eventually the planning department will learn (if only by running through the entire gamut of such fevers and chills) that an effective planning system for the company must be unique and tailored to fit its needs and aspirations.

Much more serious, and still something of a medical mystery, is an unidentified virus that attacks some planning departments in their second or third year, often with fatal results. The symptoms, minor at first, become progressively debilitating. The first sign is an increasing nervousness followed by a noticeable drop in energy which advances to a state of almost complete exhaustion; in the final stages, the department withdraws itself completely from any contact with the rest of the organization. I have visited two or three planning departments in the terminal phase of this disease, and I am convinced that it does reach an incurable stage. In our current ignorance about how to treat this illness, the only prescription seems to be a very early, radical treatment such as a shot of adrenalin from the president and/or massive transfusions of new blood into the department.[7]

Walter B. Schaffir, a planning head at Western Union elaborated on "childhood pathology" in a letter on the Vancil article:

Corporate planning infants, during their early stages of development, are often too weak to resist the "*you* claim to be a planner—give me a *plan*" virus. Succumbing to this disease leaves the planner vulnerable to ever-weakening recurrences until "his" plans lose touch entirely with the real world and become an object of ridicule. A similar weakness in the infant's stamina may often be observed in his inability to resist the "Just tell us what kind of a plan *you* want—

[7] Vancil, *op. cit.*, pp. 93–94.

we'll give it to you" virus. This disorder tends to be obscured initially by pleasant sensations. It causes planners to recklessly devise 10-step forms for the collection of mechanical response; it results in seriously retarded, and often crippled, development in adolescence.[8]

TEMPORARY UNITS

Frequently an organization does not need as much full-time, expert help as a regular planning department would offer, yet it needs more help—at least for a while—than it can expect from the present operating staff. A favorite device in this case is employment of an outside consultant, either an individual who is well recognized for his planning skills or a team of planning experts. Another favorite device is the task force. Under the leadership of a top executive, a group of men is assigned to resolve a special problem; each man is relieved temporarily from his regular duties, with the understanding that he will go back to them when the project is completed. For instance, the team's assignment may be to come up with new criteria for acquisitions of small companies or facilities, or to produce a new program of recruiting and training young managers so that planned goals will be achieved quicker, or to assess the opportunities presented by a new market or a new invention and, if they seem promising, propose a course of action for the chief executive to consider.

SPECIALIZED TEAMS

Finally, the organization may feel that it needs the help of a permanently established unit—but a fairly specialized type of help from this unit, not assistance on any and all kinds of planning problems (as would be provided by the full-fledged planning department earlier described). This kind of staff has become quite common in American industry and is seen repeatedly in education, government, and the military. Although it is sometimes called a "planning department," it characteristically limits itself to a narrow range of tasks, doing them "in depth" and with an

[8] *Harvard Business Review*, September–October, 1967, p. 35.

expertise that could not be expected of regular employees who have to worry about keeping operations and programs moving.

For instance, a few years ago the Grocery Products Division of General Mills, Inc., set up a new product and planning department to help the division heads plan. This department worked on finding ideas for new products, coordinating certain activities of the division with what the corporation's central research department was doing, and controlling and scheduling the development of new products. But the division's controller was the one who was responsible for preparing and carrying out long- and short-term plans; his leadership in this area was in no way challenged by the new product and planning department. (On his office wall, the director of this department displayed this sign: "Developing new product ideas is like making love to an elephant. If you're successful nothing happens for at least two years. If you're not you get trampled to death.")[9]

In another division of General Mills, the Chemical Division, a different kind of unit was organized. Here again the main planning jobs were carried out by various top executives of the division. Where they felt they needed special help was in the mechanics of planning and the coordination of different executives' programs. Hence they set up a planning and analysis group consisting of a manager and four analysts. This group, too, reported to the controller of the division.[10]

As for Time, Inc., it too, had a special unit, despite its strong insistence that planning be done by operating people. This unit was called "Corporate Development." Half of its members were full-time specialists, half were on loan from various divisions. The unit concentrated on making studies of such subjects as new technologies of communication, information storage and retrieval, and certain industries like newspapers and phonograph records; it also evaluated companies that Time might want to buy. The head

[9] General Mills, Inc., a case copyrighted in 1967 by the President and Fellows of Harvard College (ICH 12C5, BC 289, Harvard Business School), p. 9.
[10] Ibid., p. 11.

of Corporate Development emphasized that the department had nothing to do with the company's three-year plans coordinated by the comptroller's office.[11]

UNDERLYING FACTORS

Reflecting on the varying needs for assistance which different organizations have, the astute observer will note that much depends on two factors: (1) the degree of centralization or decentralization and (2) the maturity of formal planning. For instance, in business a company with a very decentralized form of organization (typically a corporation with many divisions, each of which produces for a different market or industry) is likely to assign its planning department to an information-gathering role, at least at first. The primary need of corporate leaders is to get a clear picture of divisional plans (or absence of plans), and management has no interest in a planning group that goes beyond that limited task. Once such a picture is gained, however, the planning department may be given a more advanced assignment: matching divisional programs to corporate resources and, in particular, helping to tie the strategies of divisions into the grand strategy of top management for the corporation as a whole. In this more advanced stage of evolution the planning department may be called on to give a more sophisticated kind of help than in the early stages.

On the other hand, in a company that produces just a few kinds of products or services (e.g., an airline or a retail chain) the planning department is likely to find itself participating right at the outset in the formulation of corporate strategy. It will be given the job of making the financial analyses management depends on, developing assumptions about the future, evaluating major alternatives, and in other ways sharing in the preparation of major plans and programs.

Some fairly clear patterns of this kind emerged from a study done in 1968 by several students at the Harvard Business School.

[11] Time, Incorporated, *op. cit.*, p. 2.

The students, A. C. Dix, W. E. Kaffenberger, and J. L. Withers, studied the development of formal planning systems in eight American companies: General Mills, Time, American Airlines, Raytheon, J. C. Penney, Caterpillar, Norton, and Cities' Service.

Generating a Climate of Change

The formal assignment of planning responsibilities to certain executives and staff groups is only one dimension of the organization job. A second dimension has to do with measures to stimulate thinking about change and innovation regardless of the scope of planning being attempted or of the way in which assignments are parceled out. In a sense this latter dimension is more fundamental. It affects the mood and tenor of the whole organization —its receptivity to new ideas, its interest in experimenting, its willingness to follow new leaders along new paths. Without the right "climate," the most carefully devised organization schemes will wither away and become meaningless; on the other hand, an organization possessing the right to climate can make many kinds of formal setup look good. Accordingly we must give special attention to efforts to stimulate, through organization, a favorable climate of change. If one purpose of organization is to increase the chances for spontaneity, then such efforts are designed to increase spontaneity where it counts the most.

MEETINGS FOR PROBLEM IDENTIFICATION

Some planning leaders have had good luck with meetings in which the purpose is not to try to answer questions and solve problems, but to *ask* important questions and *describe* troublesome situations. This technique was used with success by the vice-president for manufacturing of an electric appliance company. He scheduled weekly meetings between himself and his five leading subordinates. At these meetings he allowed problems to be identified but insisted that any efforts to solve them be deferred to other meetings. To encourage preparation for these meetings, he asked subordinates to come in with brief oral reports. He encouraged each of them to pursue the same general approach with their own groups of assistants, and he rated them partly on how well they seemed to do in this respect.

REVIEW OF RESEARCH

At one leading United States corporation, a group of key men (all connected in some way with long-range planning) meet monthly to go over the principal R&D programs in process in various parts of the company. To help the committee members become familiar with various divisions and their plans, each meeting is held at a different location in the company. The company also conducts seminars for senior technical executives and their engineers in which papers are presented reviewing developments in various areas of research that might influence corporate planning.

Numerous variations of this basic approach can be found in other companies. All serve the human side of planning by keeping organizational leaders alert to new technical developments and their possible implications for the future—by fostering, in effect, a kind of "self-renewal" among managers. One company, Standard Oil of Indiana, takes the process a step further. A formal reporting system has been set up between the central research laboratory and the various divisions, with the purpose of maintaining continuous two-way communication concerning needs and ideas for research, priorities, progress on projects under way, and other aspects.[12]

"KEEPING UP" WITH THE OUTSIDE WORLD

Self-renewal can also be served by monitoring pertinent trends and developments in outside organizations. To this end, the heads

[12] See Lawrence D. McGlauchlin, "Long-Range Technical Planning," *Harvard Business Review*, July–August, 1968, p. 54.

of many military, government, and corporate organizations make sure that certain of their key men attend conventions, association meetings, and technical sessions in which new ideas are likely to be offered in fields of interest (e.g., innovations in urban transit, for city planners, or new techniques of investment analysis, for a mutual fund).

In industry—and also, of course, in the military—one of the most interesting activities is gaining intelligence on competitors. One company proceeds as follows: Management assigns each young executive to one of the firm's many competitors. His job is to learn as much about that competitor as he can, drawing mainly on published data since he cannot leave his regular job for long periods of "sleuthing." At the annual budget presentations for his division he is asked what he would be doing during the next few years if he were the head of the competing company. For instance, he might be giving a real push to sales of product X, or buying a small company to give him more strength in developing product Y, or selling his warehouses and going out of business in area Z. His report may show that certain assumptions in the division's budget need to be changed.

Not to be overlooked is the possible value of monitoring new developments in customer and supplier organizations. For instance, James Brian Quinn reports that one company—a seller of industrial goods—assigns a marketing research group to keep in touch with those in prospect firms who do long-range planning. The research group helps the prospective customer spot future needs and opportunities, and, on the basis of information brought back, the company plans part of its own development efforts.[13]

In the consumer goods field a number of companies support what are called "grass roots" research programs, viz., use of first-line salesmen to collect data on trends in the marketplace and use of other field marketing personnel to analyze and interpret the data. This dual involvement of field staffs helps to develop

[13] See Quinn's chapter, "Top Management Guides for Research Planning," in James R. Bright (ed.), *Technological Planning on the Corporate Level* (Boston, Harvard Business School, 1962).

strong links between forecasted conditions and day-to-day marketing decisions; also, of course, it helps to give management early warning of shifts in consumer preferences.

MUSTERING SUPPORT FOR NEW PROJECTS

Once new ideas are known and once new needs for programs are assessed, the question arises: How much support, if any, will the organization give to the projects? All too often the answer is negative—token support, lip service, or perhaps open opposition. I have been told again and again, for instance, of organizations in government and industry that have set up boards and committees to listen to proposals for innovation and to select the best ones for financial backing. What do the boards and committees do? They kill every proposal that comes before them! To protect the "establishment" from interference with projects it is already working on, the new-idea committees screen out 100 percent of the proposals for innovations. To the extent that this is done, the climate of change and spontaneity is worsened, and planning is the ultimate loser no matter how well it is executed in other respects. The following are given as examples of action taken by various companies to assure that innovators and innovations in the organization *do* get proper support.

A successful science-based firm in Boston helps generate the innovative spirit throughout the organization by means of a research advisory board. This board is made up of outsiders—leading scientists from universities and foundations. It meets regularly to hear new ideas conceived by scientists, engineers, and managers in the company's employ. The ideas are presented informally, and often in an early state of formation. The advisory board reacts to them with such judgments as "Sounds good but you should check what Batelle has been doing in this line," or "We don't see how you would get around this problem," or "Maybe you've really got something there; keep working on it and come back to us next month." Not infrequently, of course, the board will discourage the idea because of knowledge of un-

successful trials elsewhere. Because the board members are outsiders and have no vested interest in current projects and operations and also because part of their personal reward for serving
(they get a fee, of course) is exposure to fresh thinking, their
relationship with members of the company staff tends to be a
creative, inventive one.

Another company uses an advisory board to help keep top
executives creative *as administrators and policy-makers*. This advisory board is composed of leading executives from other organizations. Their job is to review periodically what top management is doing, how it is doing it, what kinds of problems it is
experiencing, and so forth—with the aim of acting not only as
an auditor but also as a prodder and catalyst. This company is
a small one and, thanks in part to its board, very profitable.

Perhaps the most ambitious (and expensive) organizational invention for supporting new ideas is the so-called development department or new ventures division. A leading proponent of this
approach is E. I. duPont de Nemours & Company. DuPont was
troubled by the tendency of operating managers in established divisions to become preoccupied with products and processes that
were already successful or in which they had already invested
much time, research, and planning. Yet in the research departments of these divisions new ideas were continually being conceived. Who would be willing to take these ideas, appraise them
sympathetically, invest money in them if they looked commer-
cially promising, get a staff of people to produce and market
them—in short, nurture them to the point at which operating divisions *would* find them attractive to adopt?

DuPont's answer was to set up its development department.
This department's assignment is to be entrepreneurial from start
to finish; once a new product or process it sponsors has succeeded
in its market tests, it is passed on to a newly created or established operating department. In one sense, what DuPont seeks is
the small-company entrepreneurial spirit within the walls of a
mammoth corporation. In another sense, though, it seeks to outdo
the small company. When the small company succeeds with a

new product, it usually gets into commercial manufacturing and marketing and then loses the inventive spirit it had at the beginning. DuPont's aim is to keep the creative flame of those early stages continually burning in the development division.

Although this division is young, it appears to be proving its worth. Chances are good that the concept will be borrowed in the future by many other companies, including much smaller ones than DuPont. Other corporations that have already tested such an approach include Minnesota Mining & Manufacturing Company. Its new products division is assigned to develop items that might not fit in any regular division. As at DuPont, projects are handed over to operating divisions when development success is achieved.

Because of the success of advisory boards, development departments, and other such ambitious approaches, one may be inclined to overlook the potentials of relatively simple and "homemade" devices to encourage innovation. Those potentials are great. The example I recommend is that of an extraordinary executive in a nationally known manufacturer of consumer soft goods. It is his conviction that screening boards and committees should reflect a policy of being penny-foolish and pound-wise.

In his branch of company operations the policy used to be to invest in relatively few new product ideas. The proposals would go through a long series of screening processes, and the ones that were best analyzed, argued, and presented would then go off the drawing boards into market testing. He dropped that policy in favor of a new approach that, he believes, leads to more and better innovative projects. If a new product or merchandising proposal passes its *initial* screen tests now, the proponents are given a small budget for building prototypes, making market tests, or whatever else is needed to find out what happens when consumers actually see the item. Only after that is a more formal, top-level review made of the proposed project.

The new procedure has these advantages: (1) Executives do not get so committed to the idea, before large funds are spent on it, that they feel they cannot back out of it. Under the old system, by the time proponents had weathered all the committee screenings and reviews, they often came to feel so emotionally committed to the idea that they could not regard market tests objectively. (2) Even the most experienced executives are often surprised at consumer reactions to a new item. The new procedure provides earlier signs that sales judgments may be right or wrong. (3) Long, elaborate, review-and-analysis procedures tend to favor the more articulate members of the company. Yet such people are not always the ones who have the best proposals from a marketing standpoint. (4) Also, the executive says, the more conventional and elaborate review-and-analysis procedures tend, unless checked, to "formalize procrastination."

A Perspective

It is tempting to overstress the role of organizational devices in getting planning done and creating the right climate for it. Too often experts on organization convey the impression that a certain shuffling of responsibilities, a carving out of new authorities, a new set of job descriptions will lead—presto!—to fabulous results. Of course, that is not true. An organization scheme does not make a company, army, college, or agency successful any more than a planning scheme does. It is people (as we have stressed) who make the enterprise successful.

But this truth does not negate the value of organization. Rather, it reinforces it—at least, if an organization scheme or procedure is seen as an aid to planning and decision-making, an aid that is useful only insofar as it is continually tailored and retailored to the ever-changing needs of the people involved. One of the greatest planners (though he did not use that word) and organizers of this century was Alfred P. Sloan, Jr. Reflecting back on his historic years with General Motors, this "old pro" wrote:

We had to start from that beginning [in the early 1900's]. It was our task to find out what forms of organization were suitable to our company. This meant, above all, an organization that could adapt to great changes in the market. Any rigidity by an automobile manufacturer, no matter how large or well established, is severely penalized in the market—as we have seen was the case with Mr. Ford in the 1920's, when he stayed too long with his old and once dominantly successful concept of the business. We had a different concept of the business, which we put into competition with his. It could have happened that he was right, but for that to have occurred, one would have to postulate the continuation of the kind of national economy that supported his concept of the automobile. As it happened, our concept was more in accord with the economy, the progress of the automobile art, and the changing interests and tastes of consumers. But after our first success, we too might have failed. There have been and always will be many opportunities to fail in the automobile industry. The circumstances of the ever-changing market and ever-changing product are capable of breaking any business organization if that organization is unprepared for change—indeed, in my opinion, if it has not provided procedures for anticipating change. . . .

In describing the General Motors organization, I hope I have not left an impression that I think it is a finished product. No company ever stops changing. Change will come for better or worse. I also hope I have not left an impression that the organization runs itself automatically. An organization does not make decisions; its function is to provide a framework, based upon established criteria, within which decisions can be fashioned in an orderly manner. Individuals make the decisions and take the responsibilty for them.[14]

THE art of getting rich consists not in industry, much less in saving, but in a better order, in timeliness, in being at the right spot.
—RALPH WALDO EMERSON

[14] *Op. cit.*, pp. 437–438 and 443.

PART IV:

Conclusion

CHAPTER 15

Some Laws of Planning

ALTHOUGH PLANNING is not a science, it appears to be subject to various "laws," just as a science is. During the hundreds of years of planning experience in different fields, certain results seem to have followed certain actions with monotonous consistency. Perhaps no tight cause-and-effect relationships can be ascribed to these actions and results, and perhaps the patterns observable in the past will not hold fast for all time to come. We must, therefore, keep our fingers crossed when referring to these patterns as "laws." Yet they would seem to serve us well in making predictions about the outcome of certain approaches to planning as we see them undertaken in different organizations.

To emphasize a point that was made at the outset of our discussion and that is especially important here, planning as we conceive it pertains to programs *for change*—change in what an organization does or in how it operates. Programs that call only for continuing what is already being done or for making only superficial changes do not come within our definition of planning. It is also worth reiterating that planning as we think of it is a *way* of dealing with the future. Planning does not mean that an organization deals with the future when otherwise it would not be doing so. In practically every business, government agency, military unit, college, and civic group, leaders regularly make decisions (or fail to make decisions) that have implications for the future of the organization. Planning comes in simply as a technique of so guiding people in the organization that their actions will affect the future in a consistent and desired way.

The modest collection of laws that follows is based in part on material in previous chapters. The pertinent chapters are noted in the discussion.

Law 1: A viable program meets the needs of (a) the formal organization, (b) individuals, and (c) groups.

The first of the three requirements is well known. It has, in fact, been the preoccupation of authorities on planning for many years. By "formal organization" we refer to the many systems and tangible resources that are essential to achieving management's purpose—production facilities, distribution, procurement, the financial system, the chain of command, and so on. The first part of this law simply says that a good program uses these systems and resources effectively to promote a purpose for which the company, agency, or institution was organized. In so doing, the program satisfies *some* of the needs that brought the people together; for example, they feel a loyalty to the organization and a desire that it perform creditably in its field.

The second and third requirements of this law are also well established but for some reason they have been commonly overlooked in the literature on planning. The law says that it is not enough for a program to be efficient in financial, manufacturing, marketing, chain-of-command, and similar terms; it must also satisfy the needs of decision-makers and action-takers as separate individuals and as members of groups. In industry, for instance, many a marketing program has been hampered by a sales manager who saw no point in extending himself to support it. He felt the program conflicted with his notion of how his work should be done or with his aspirations for status and compensation. Thus the program conflicted with his needs as an individual. In equally simple ways planning may conflict with his loyalties as a member of an informal group. For example, a new marketing head comes in and gives the sales manager a strong personal interest in supporting the program but begins demoting or dismissing a number of other executives who happen to be, like the sales manager, "old-timers" in the company. (These personnel shifts are all part of the new marketing head's program.) Therefore the wrath of the sales manager is aroused and, out of loyalty to fellow "old-timers," he begins acting in ways that seem unreasonable to the marketing director.

Sometimes people ask which of the three needs is most important. This is like asking which of the legs of a three-legged stool is most important. All of the needs are important, all are interdependent, and no one can be said to be more so than the others. During a lengthy period of time the plan cannot remain viable unless each of the needs is met adequately. In fact, Paul Lawrence, whose study of a major program for change in a retail food chain produced the first statement of the relationships just described, feels that focusing on one set of needs to the exclusion of the others can lead to a "perversion" of the project. "The perversion is created because any one-dimensional effort leads to the atrophy of the others."[1]

Corollary 1A: The perfect plan is not perfect from an organizational, individual, or group standpoint. This is because the organization, individual, and group characteristically impose conflicting demands on a program. Hence leaders have to make compromises if they are to keep the satisfaction of the three purposes in some kind of dynamic balance. The resulting plan, while not ideal from any one standpoint, meets the major needs sufficiently to make possible the achievement of real progress.

Corollary 1B: The three needs should be borne in mind during the conception and design of a program as well as during its execution. To borrow terms popularly used in the planning literature, both in strategic planning and in implementational or tactical planning it is important to observe the three-legged nature of a sound program. This will make it possible to avoid much backtracking, last-minute compromises, and desperation switches —problems that all too commonly arise when planners become

---

[1] *The Changing of Organizational Behavior Patterns, op. cit.*, p. 215.

preoccupied with one or two needs but forget the third. Also, this approach will make possible a more aggressive, positive administration of a plan. In reviewing his case study, Lawrence observed that a multi-pronged attack would have helped the executives "to maintain a sense of consistency in their behavior" and prepared them "to deal with the many sources of resistance."[2]

See chapters 3, 5, 6, 7, 8, and 12.

Law 2: Effective planning is incomplete planning.

Too much blueprinting and engineering of detail—whether "organizational" engineering or "human" engineering, to use the common appellations—has a retarding, dragging influence on a program of action rather than a lubricating influence. It may even put the kiss of death on the program. Thus, overplanning is poor planning. The following figure represents an attempt to portray this second law schematically. The exact shape of the curve would, of course, vary from situation to situation, depending on

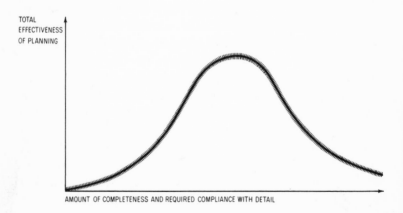

TOTAL EFFECTIVENESS OF PLANNING

AMOUNT OF COMPLETENESS AND REQUIRED COMPLIANCE WITH DETAIL

the organization's sophistication in planning, the perceived urgency of planning, the complexity of the planning problem, and

2 *Ibid.,* p. 221.

many other factors. But the general notion conveyed ought to hold up in all situations.

Why is effective planning incomplete planning? The reasons have to do with the human side and can be inferred from materials presented earlier. First, a program that is worked out to the last detail denies people down the line that which they want most—a sense of participation in the program, a piece of "the action." In an Apollo flight to the moon the astronauts are expected to act as improved robots and no detail that can be anticipated is left unattended. But this is really an engineering feat (although we may refer to it as a planning accomplishment in popular discussion). In developing goals for the Apollo program and in assigning teams of scientists, engineers, behavioral scientists, astronomers, and others to produce a vehicle and launching—this is where the real planning goes on—a great deal of discretion *is* left to the people involved, and the planning is incomplete indeed.

Second, if a program is designed to produce change, it is going to produce the unexpected somewhere along the way. Those who carry it out are going to run into novel or perhaps unheard-of problems to solve. Therefore, if the planner tries to specify in advance how to deal with the unexpected, he defeats his own purpose. An editor I know observes: "By one of those little existential ironies which keep us all on our toes, the more sophisticated the planner and the more solid and thorough his plan, the more inertia and stupidity it displays in the face of surprise, and the more it inhibits healthy responses in the individuals caught up in the surprise."

Ezra Merrill, the head of H. P. Hood & Sons, was recently asked to comment on a planning case published by the *Harvard Business Review*. The case concerned the efforts of a new chief executive to work out explicit strategies for a firm that previously had been run in a seat-of-the-pants manner by the founder. Merrill's critique is illuminating. He suggests some steps for the chief executive to take in order to get his managers thinking more about strategic planning, and he advises having some brainstorming sessions devoted to "what happens if" questions so that people down the line will begin preparations for how they themselves will deal with surprises. But Merrill is plainly against having complete blueprints made to guide managers. He comments:

> There is much magic and more than a little luck in strategic planning, and it must never be taken too seriously. By this I mean that although the exercise is essential, its quality depends upon the creative sparks that may be struck, and the planners must always be alert and hoping for the unforeseen, possibly deflecting circumstance that will enrich their output beyond their planned planning at its best.[3]

Corollary 2A: The optimum amount of detail is roughly proportional to the organization's experience in planning. If the agency or company is still new to planning, the peak of the curve in Figure 1 should be moved to the left. Such an organization can have neither skills nor a built-up tolerance for planning, so planners must "go slow" with both the scope and content of programs for change. Robert Schaffer of Robert Schaffer & Associates in Stamford, Connecticut, is the leading exponent of this view. In a wide variety of situations—hospitals, small firms, large companies, and other organizations that are "getting their feet wet" for the first time—he has demonstrated how much more effective planning is if it begins with immediate problems, the concerns of today rather than tomorrow. Then and only then does the organization begin to develop the capacity to reach out for more ambitious strategies and programs of change.

Corollary 2B: The less able and trustworthy a planning leader's subordinates, the less he can plan in any way. This is because he must watch and direct the activities of such subordinates so closely that he cannot allow them the discretion necessary if he is to direct a large or ambitious program. The strongest argument for Douglas McGregor's "Theory Y"—the liberal, fairly generous approach to sharing of authority—is that it either forces organization leaders to give subordinates a "piece of the action" or to hire subordinates who *can* be trusted with discretion, thus creating one condition essential to vigorous planning. By the same

[3] See Robert Mainer, "The Case of the Slippery Strategy," May–June, 1968, p. 180.

token, the most damaging criticism of "Theory X"—the rigid, regimented, tight-control philosophy—is the drain it creates on possibilities for planning.[4]

(It is worth noting, by the way, that the reverse of this corollary is not true. For instance, the astronauts in an Apollo moon mission are as able and trustworthy people as can be found, yet their mission must be largely "programmed" rather than planned. This is because the relatively small number of surprises they run into are so crucial.)

See chapters 3, 11, and 13.

Law 3: Every well-drawn plan is out of date by the time it is in use.

This is because every organization in modern society is continuously changing. Conditions around it are changing, its problems are varying, the people in it are getting younger or older, and so on. Accordingly, if a plan is perfectly tailored to conditions at the time it is drawn up, it will be somewhat out of tune even before the first effort can be made to implement it. If it is made to suit conditions as anticipated five years hence, it is also out of date after the first week because not every condition can possibly be anticipated correctly and the chain of events leading to the error is already in motion.

The validity of this law rests not alone on the human or material realities of planning but on the interaction between the two sides. Duncan E. Littlefair observes: "Life is not something that builds systematically, adding a piece here and there. If you touch any one part of an organism, you touch the whole of it. You make one little change and you change the whole body in some degree."[5] This applies to organizations as well as to individuals.

The planning movement in industrialized nations would be ad-

---

[4] Douglas McGregor, *The Human Side of Enterprise* (New York, Mc-Graw-Hill Book Company, Inc., 1961).

[5] "The More Things Change," Fountain Street Church, Grand Rapids, Michigan, February 25, 1968.

vanced considerably if this chronic limitation of planning could be more widely appreciated. How far back Utopian hopes for planning date, I do not know—probably to the early nineteenth century, if not before. In any event, they linger on, handicapping the planner by placing impossible burdens on him. "I am perennially saddened," wrote Arthur D. Trottenberg, once a faculty planner for Harvard University, "by the never-ending yearning for an 'over-all plan'—that wonderful, permanent ordering of people, money, space, and buildings, in which everyone will have an Eames chair, a parking space, and the trains will always, always run on time."[6]

Corollary 3A: The only plan that conceivably can be 100 percent up to date is one that was drawn in error. For instance, planning leaders may have *thought* that a cost reduction of 10 percent was realistic; it was not realistic in truth at that time and no change of circumstances was anticipated, but the unexpected may have happened so that a 10 percent cut indeed came within the realm of reason.

See chapters 2 and 3.

Law 4: Planning creates antiplanning.

The very acts of planning, even highly skilled planning and additional planning efforts after the process has become established, create new "units" of antiplanning. These "units" are not measurable, and therefore the term must be used metaphorically, but the situation is not unlike Newton's law of physics stating that for every force there is an equal and opposite reaction; that is, for every planning force that might be found to exist there is an opposite reaction or antiplanning force. One might well speculate that, were we able to measure this force, it would be found to be equal as well as opposite to the planning force.

While we cannot measure the antiplanning reaction, we know it exists. Common forms of evidence are man-made delays to much-needed programs, hostility to new acts of planning, hostility to planners, vague manifestations of discontent with a

[6] *Harvard Alumni Bulletin,* November 7, 1964.

program, unreasonable lapses in administering it, unexpected resignations—symptoms which, to be sure, can frequently be attributed to planning errors or mismanagement, but not always, and which therefore must sometimes represent more basic phenomena, since they always seem to exist and never seem to be eliminated.

In an earlier chapter we saw several reasons why employees resist planning—fear of its implications, reluctance to leave operating routines, and concern over the risks entailed ,in new programs. Even if these sentiments did not exist, antiplanning would still be produced because of basic instincts in human nature. Three in particular should be noted. First, a member of an organization draws attention to himself by reacting negatively to positive acts of planning. His opposition is a subtle method of asserting his individuality. Depending on his maturity and self-understanding, he may suppress the temptation to oppose and, for all practical purposes, cooperate vigorously on planning projects. Nevertheless, he feels the negative reaction and harbors it in some manner. It may come out some day in some unrelated form, such as a dislike of organizational life, or a desire for a change of jobs, or animosity to some person.

Second, a negative reaction to a positive act of planning satisfies the natural urge to hurt the planning leader. It is a way of "getting back" at him; it is a weapon. Again, the reaction may be internalized so completely that it does not interfere with cooperation—but it will come out in some manner, at some time, and the very act of harboring it provides a kind of satisfaction. (This desire to hurt is, of course, quite analogous to the desire to hurt a parent, friend, or loved one, which every psychologist knows.)

Third, negative reactions to new acts of planning satisfy the desire to avoid responsibility and to escape the tensions that go with responsibility. Management imposes great burdens on the individual who becomes involved in it, and planning as an advanced method of management places especially great burdens on him. Even the finest manager rebels against these burdens from time to time. The explosions may not release all of his "anti-feelings" against planning or more than a fraction of them; if they do not, his feelings will surely be channeled in some other form.

Some readers will recognize a kinship between the foregoing and the "death wish" as explained by psychologists and philosophers. The rationale just presented is in fact adapted from psychology. Underlying antiplanning is the same deep-down proneness for extinction and tragedy which has been observed in many aspects of human relations. Antiplanning is simply the death wish applied to organizational life; without planning the organization is more easily victimized in a hard world. We do not understand this death wish, Littlefair points out. He adds:

> We offer some solutions in terms of our myth to explain our guilt, but there is in man as a natural creature something which responds to extinction, lower levels, and death. The heights to which we climbed are perilous heights, and they require all the drive and energy and intelligence we can muster to maintain them. We get tired and we seek ever lower levels. There is in man something that wants to go back to that from which he came, the great unknown, undistinguishable sea of unconsciousness.[7]

Nowhere are the heights to which Littlefair refers more perilous than in modern organization, with the relentless demands it imposes on the individual for productivity, improvement, aggressiveness—and, at the same time, for social cooperation and self-discipline.

In passing, it should be added that the opposite of this fourth law does not hold; that is, antiplanning does not create planning.

See chapters 4 and 12.

Law 5: The planning leader who is effective for a sustained period has political power.

If the planning leader is not able to get others to do what he wants them to do (which is what we mean by power), planning cannot amount to very much in the organization for very long. Even though it satisfies some of man's loftiest ambitions—to

[7] "Strange Defeat," Fountain Street Church, Grand Rapids, Michigan, January 14, 1968.

create, to achieve, to find self-fulfillment, to live with the excitement of challenge—it poses too much of a threat to the status quo and "the establishment" to survive on its own merits as an idea. Planning can have only sporadic victories without power backing. For instance, the members of an organization may voluntarily subscribe to it during a period of crisis or while under the spell of a planning leader who is a supersalesman. But once the crisis or spell is over, planning is over.

Therefore, to predict the future role and prospects of planning in a company, agency, or army, you must determine who is the planning *leader* (that is, the highest-ranking person who will spend substantial time and energy on working out goals and programs and seeing to their execution). If he is a person with substantial political power, then you can safely predict an influential role for planning if he uses the power knowledgeably. But if he is a person who lacks such power—who operates principally out of an advisory or consulting type of capacity, for instance, or who has a large office and status but cannot "move" other decision-makers—then you can take a dim view of the potential of planning in that organization. You can do this even though the planning leader occupies an impressive box on the organization chart and is bright, perceptive, knowledgeable, and dedicated.

See chapters 9, 10, 12, 13, and 14.

Law 6: Good planning does not always succeed.

The reason is that there are too many other "variables," too many events outside the planner's power which can overturn or upset the most astutely laid out program. In fact, we could go further and state that planning *should not* always succeed. Good plans accept risks; therefore some are doomed to fail. If an organization has a 100 percent batting average in accomplishing many programs, you can be fairly sure it took no risks and hence is not in the "big leagues" of planning.

Corollary 6A: Poor planning does not always fail. A program may be based on some untenable assumptions; parts of it may be utterly inconsistent; the thinking behind it may be amateurish. But all such errors will be forgiven in the history books if fate is kind enough to the venture.

A classic case in point is William the Conquerer's invasion of England. If, early in September of 1066, William had investigated the naval defenses organized by King Harold of England, he would have found a formidable navy patrolling the Channel. That navy, which had been patrolling all summer in anticipation of an invasion from Normandy, could have wrought havoc on William's fleet. Obviously, as part of his planning, William *should* have sent out many scouts and ascertained in detail how King Harold's navy was operating. But he did not do this; he simply got his invasion under way as soon as he could without checking ahead at all. His army landed in England on September 25 without harassment because, quite unknown to him, Harold's ships had sailed back to London and other home ports shortly before. Harold, it seems, had let his navy go home because it was bored with inactivity and threatening to revolt; also, delays in launching the Norman invasion had led Harold to believe erroneously that William had called his plan off. William had none of this intelligence when he sailed. (In other respects, though, as we saw earlier, William did his planning well.)

See chapters 2 and 4.

Law 7: The act of planning itself changes the situation in which the organization operates.

This law, which often defies all logic and baffles the analytical mind, can be demonstrated at practically any time in a work group or enterprise of practically any size. It means that managers can alter conditions that affect the progress of their programs —can actually change the odds of success—by involving people in such routine planning activities as discussing what programs are desirable, pondering who should carry out the programs and when, gathering data for such questions, leading the organization to reach an understanding about goals and programs, and leading people to make personal commitments to projects.

This seventh law refers to the fact that if people are convinced a certain goal is attainable, they will find ways of attaining it which seem to them to be worth working on, no matter how futile the ways may seem to every one else. If they come to believe a certain program of action is promising, they will find the hard work of preparation for it rewarding, no matter how ridiculous such preparation seemed to them before they became sold on the program. If they believe that certain individuals can be entrusted with more responsibility, as a means of making a plan work, they will see more evidence of responsibility in the manner the individuals go about doing their work, even though wise observers who lack such a conviction see no such evidence in the individuals' work patterns.

Of course, there is nothing new about this insight; it has gone under such well-known labels as the "self-fulfilling prophecy" or the "self-validating belief." What is not so well recognized is that it applies with particular force to planning. By its nature, planning involves changing people's images of reality and changing their visions of the future. People see their organization, their associates, the opportunities for their groups in the ways they want to see them, and planning is a method of altering such wants. People influence the destiny of their organization by the attitudes and concerns they adopt, and planning is a method of "selling" certain attitudes and concerns.

In a sense, this law of planning is the most remarkable one. It means that leaders can lift themselves by their own bootstraps —advance themselves toward the goal at least a little bit simply by changing, through planning, their own and others' perceptions of reality and possibility. Later it may be found that the plan was in error, or mistakes and events later on may make it unattainable, but even then the failure is likely to be perceived differently because of the initial acts of planning. Some of the most tragic and erroneous planning in history managed, for all of its mistakes, to make a sizable dent on the world precisely for this reason, because the processes in which people were led to participate changed their perceptions of work purpose, reality, and failure. Witness the conviction that for so long drove the

Red Chinese to achieve Mao's goals and made them oblivious to hundreds of signs of the futility, unworkability, and unreality of his programs.

A happier example is a United States military venture that accomplished a seemingly impossible objective in the face of numerous obstacles. I asked several leaders of the venture how much of their astounding success could be credited to planning. "Some but not much," they answered. "Our planning wasn't always good, and we were always changing it." Then they thought further and reconsidered. "But planning made us 'think positive,'" they added, "and that was everything. We worked back from a target in small steps to see what had to be done, and then we looked at one step at a time and decided we could do it if we stretched. We became convinced we couldn't fail." Planning so altered their perceptions that they confidently launched into a task that was "impossible" to complete! Many astounding feats by industrial enterprises could be explained in nearly identical terms.

See chapters 7, 8, and 12.

Future Breakthrough

The coming breakthrough in planning will be on the human side. It will come because planning leaders insist on approaching the human side in the same basic manner that they have learned to approach the material and contractual sides.

In finance, production, distribution, industrial relations, and related areas, planning has been used by organization leaders as a tool for bringing themselves and their staffs into closer grips with reality. Planning has been employed as a tool for analyzing prospects and possibilities, for showing what realistically needs to be done to advance a desired distance in a desired direction. The financial executive does not generalize, "I guess we can get enough money to support this planned expansion of plant and facilities," which he might have done without the planning discipline. Rather, he talks with company people and lenders; he projects probable cash flows, interest rates, liabilities, contingencies, and other factors; he uses formulas, computers, and perhaps simulation; he maps out on a month-to-month basis whether the company *in fact* will probably be able to finance the proposed expansion.

By contrast, on the human side we have tended to follow the primitive way, satisfying ourselves with such pat generalities as "a plan that's good for the company is good for all employees" or "our people will be under pressure but they'll produce if we explain the problem." Such bland generalizations shield the planning leader from the human facts just as "I guess we can get enough money" would shield him from vital financial facts. The human side must be analyzed. Which individuals and which groups will be approached? When and in what order? In what manner and with what types of incentives and pressures? Where will the likely "people problems" be, and what decisions might we make now that could alleviate or aggravate those problems? What does the experience of other organizations and enterprises teach us about planning in such-and-such a manner?

Such an analytical approach to the human side offers no guarantee of success with a venture. What it offers is assurance that realities will be grasped better—ideally, a much wider range and depth of realities than would be thought possible without planning. For this is what planning is about: thinking ahead in terms of realities instead of fantasies. The aggressive organization today can choose from an endlessly varied assortment of real opportunities. In almost every world of affairs now—in industry, in education, in government, in health and welfare—the area is large enough so that organizations in it can be whatever they want to be.

THE battle of Waterloo was won on the playing fields of Eton.
—ARTHUR WELLESLEY, DUKE OF WELLINGTON

Index

9